WOODSTOCK VISION

THE BAND

van morrison moondance

SELF-PORTRAIT '78

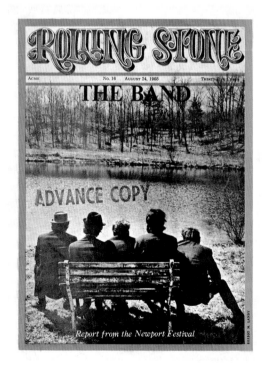

ELLIOTT LANDY

WOODSTOCK VISION

THE SPIRIT OF A GENERATION

INCLUDING SELECTIONS FROM

WOODSTOCK 69, THE FIRST FESTIVAL

A LANDYVISION BOOK — WOODSTOCK, NY

Backbeat Books

AN IMPRINT OF HAL LEONARD CORPORATION
NEW YORK

To Joiwind and Bo for being my children and bringing me such joy.
To Lynda, my wife, whom I have always loved.
To my sisters, Rita and Barbara, for their love and support.
To Steven, Valeree, Gregg, and Christine, my new children,
and Julia and Thea, my dreams for the future.

Backbeat Books
An Imprint of Hal Leonard Corporation
7777 West Bluemound Road
Milwaukee, WI 53213

Trade Book Division Editorial Offices
19 West 21st Street, New York, NY 10010

Revised edition published in 2009

Portions of this book were originally published as *Woodstock Vision: The Spirit of a Generation* by Continuum
International Publishing Group in 1994 and *Woodstock 1969: The First Festival: 3 Days of Peace & Music—A
Photo Commemorative* by Squarebooks in 1994.

Graphic design by Tony Fradkin
Photo arrangements by Elliott Landy
All photographs, interviews, and text by Elliott Landy except as noted above

Printed in China

Library of Congress Cataloging-in-Publication Data
is available upon request.

ISBN 978-0-87930-965-7

www.backbeatbooks.com

Elliott Landy's website: www.Landyvision.com

Dedication

I love photography. It has always been good to me. It has taken me to the places I wanted to go, helped me meet some of the people I wanted to meet, and allowed me to share with others some of my deepest experiences.

I was lucky. In the early days of my career I chose to photograph people and events that later came to be socially and culturally significant. But when I was photographing Jim Morrison in the Hunter College Auditorium, or Janis Joplin in the Anderson Theater on New York's Lower East Side, neither event had, then or now, any meaning for me beyond my momentary love of the music they were creating and the way they looked creating it. The thrill, the inspiration of the moment was all there was. To capture a flickering moment of joyous experience and share it with others — that was the reason I began photographing in the first place, and that is still the reason I take pictures today. I was never a fan.

In between the beginning and now, the chance to earn a living at what I loved to do occurred and so I took it and kept taking it, and to this sort of chance in life, I dedicate this book.

Try to be happy, try to have fun, and try to share this happiness and fun with those around you, and may God (the universal experience) expand your conception of happiness to include helping those near you who need help. And may communication bring all of us on this planet closer together, closer to God, closer to each other.

Elliott Landy
Woodstock,
New York
August 1994

THE AUTHOR, 1970

The Vision of a Generation

There was a terrible war raging in Vietnam in the Sixties. We, the Woodstock Generation, knew it was wrong and fought against it. We didn't care what the social penalties were — we stood our ground and said, "No, this is wrong. I love my country and will not participate in this immoral action which destroys the principles on which our country was built."

At the same time, music was reaching us. It got us so excited that we felt a deep part of ourselves which we had not been in touch with before. It was wild, and its wildness freed us from cultural restraints, from the uptightness that habits place on a human being. So people were free to be naked in public, to talk about having sex, to smoke grass openly with friends, take acid, have long hair, dress any way they chose, to experiment and explore life freely.

I was a young photographer looking for a way to publish my work. I was a human being, hurt and injured by the injustice of the war. I was a person who smoked grass occasionally and loved to listen to music. When I was stoned, I always wanted to take pictures. I combined all these elements into an attempt to make my life good. I wanted to earn money, make beautiful pictures, listen to music, and help the world.

Everything seemed to be changing. Established ideas and institutions, in every sphere, were being challenged. It seemed like the world was about to change profoundly because people would not be able to go on living the way they had been. It was a time of hope.

The frontiers of consciousness were being expanded. We were exposed to Eastern philosophy, metaphysical books, psychedelics, rock music, and grass.

Rock concerts were rites of passage, where people came to be together, to see the bands, and to get high from the music, the dance, and the drugs. The goal was to transcend the mundane vision of everyday life by reaching an ecstatic state. We were unknowingly using methods similar to those found in the traditions of indigenous peoples throughout history.

Pop music had not yet become an international business and cultural phenomenon. Rock 'n' roll was outside the norm of society, part of the "underground" culture, and to be involved with it made you an outsider. A new group of people who believed in alternatives to the American Way of Life was galvanized by this new, free form of raucous music. A world of hippies, drugs, free love, metaphysics, and political activism was born.

The musicians themselves could as easily have been members of the audience as performers onstage, and often they did mingle with the crowds after the show. There was a true feeling of solidarity, a unity of purpose, and the purpose was to change the world. "We want the world, and we want it NOW!" was the anthem sung by Jim Morrison. We thought that the freedom to behave as we wished, coupled with the power of music to liberate the soul, would emancipate the world.

The Sixties were about trying to discover the truth about everything and trying to live that truth in life. Discovering your inner self, and being true to it. Doing what you really wanted to do, and trusting that if you did the right thing, "your way" would be in alignment with The Way, (as in the ancient Chinese text The Way of Life) and the universe would support you by making the right things happen for you. People tried to earn the money they needed from "work" they loved.

The Sixties were also about looking for happiness and trying to create perfection and justice for everyone on the planet. For the first time a mass culture saw itself as totally interconnected to all other beings and began to take on a global rather than a local responsibility. The tools we used were love, freedom, spirituality, music, and action. We demanded freedoms long held to be taboo—to have sex at will, to use consciousness-expanding substances—and we actively tried to change the establishment through righteous, inspired action.

A lot of other things changed as well. Before the Sixties, men had short hair and crew cuts and wore business suits and ties. Social conformity prevented them from wearing frilly shirts and earrings. But the Sixties emancipated men's creative and feminine side. Freedom replaced formality. Men not only

THE WHO, FILLMORE EAST THEATER, '68

let their hair and beards grow and put on more colorful clothes, they also smiled more lovingly and became more accepting of others. So many people were naked that men began to accept real women's bodies instead of focusing on Playboy fantasies. They concentrated more on feelings and emotions than on physical satisfaction—something only women had done before. Women and men became better friends. Instead of guys just hanging out together, talking dirty, and harassing women, a new situation arose: men and women hung out together, smoked dope, had sex, and listened to rock 'n' roll. A communal experience was born. Men began cooking and taking care of children, while women got into rock 'n' roll.

Thus the education and upbringing of children began to change. Children were carried around with their parents, brought to parties, and learned to sleep in a car. Home was any place where the road stopped. Children no longer stayed home with baby-sitters; parents started, more and more, to bring their kids with them, and the kids were much better off.

Drugs were a part of that interconnectedness, but they were light, nonaddicting, consciousness-raising natural herbs, which helped us attain higher states. Unlike hyperaggressive drugs, such as cocaine, they made us more mellow, more loving, more sensitive, and more open.

Grass was special — you shared it. We had been taught to keep our possessions to ourselves, but when you smoked grass, you offered it to whoever happened to be nearby, whether you were in the street or at a rock concert. Being "high" opened people up to themselves and to others. Smoking was a communal activity and often created an instant bonding, even if it sometimes lasted only a short time.

Since you were more mellow when you were "high," you were able to listen and to perceive more. You could really 'get into another person's trip,' sit and play with a baby for hours, or "see" a flower for what seemed like the first time. In some ways drugs worked similarly to meditation, reducing the perceptual blocks and illusions of separateness we learned from our Western cultural upbringing.

One of the main visions which permeated the Sixties culture was of the brotherhood of man. Many people were initially able to perceive this truth because of grass and other consciousness-enhancing drugs.

The Woodstock Generation rediscovered many ancient spiritual truths and gave the contemporary world an alternative vision for living —to be loving, gentle, and open all the time. Drugs were a window to that vision, but there was a price to pay. When drugs are used to reach the highs, one is less capable of dealing graciously with the lows and responds negatively to situations that could be handled better. Reactions such as anger, depression, physical depletion, and dependency are common. The ultimate goal is to be able to experience and enjoy life: the freedom and the ecstasy of being in a loving state of mind, and the strength to experience the difficulties without being upset, uptight, or anxious.

Now we realize that we must reach that state, not through harmful chemicals, but through meditation and inner spiritual commitment to joy and love, coupled with the hard work of getting through life while maintaining our integrity.

SWAMI SATCHTANANDA, WOODSTOCK FESTIVAL

We hoped to leave the existing society behind and do our own thing—find our own truths and way of life. The Sixties culture called for a rejection of material and traditional comforts. We no longer needed beds to sleep in. The floor and a mat would do. Insurance plans, new cars, new clothes, traditional ceremonies, nine-to-five jobs, meaningless work done just to pay the bills—all were questioned and discarded.

What was important was to get high, to feel yourself, to become one with the spiritual forces in the universe, to communicate with our fellow man. So what if we lived in houses that would never be ours, drove cars that were falling apart, wore clothes that were used when we got them? As long as we shared what we had with each other, we would be all right. We felt we could live a nomadic, transient life as long as we were loving and generous.

We also thought meaningless middle-class values would disappear. Little did we realize then that in every historical phase there is a dialectic in which first one, then an opposite action predominates, followed by a synthesis of the two.

The yuppies of the Eighties, with their total focus on material wealth and meaningless status symbols, were a reaction to the drop-out, turn-on, tune-in hippie culture of the Sixties.

The energy created during that time is still with us, slowly influencing us more and more. It has evolved into what is today called New Age thought. The inheritors of "Woodstock" are not only the tie-dyed young people we see at concerts, but also the healers, the spiritual practitioners, and the activists who support the diversity of planetary life-forms. Many young people are intuitively drawn to the Woodstock era, feeling a closeness they don't yet fully understand while taking inspiration from its lifestyles.

Perhaps the Twenty-first century will be a time of synthesis for the two ways of thinking and being, for balancing a spiritual awareness of our place in the universe with an ability to work toward making physical life on this planet more pleasant for everyone. What we of the Sixties generation have learned is that the material part of life is important as well. As the I Ching says, the ultimate manifestation of Heaven is on Earth.

8

Stars and Stones

In 1967 a lot of things were wrong with America and I felt I had to say something about what was going on. I wanted to take pictures that explained the truth to people and presented them with alternatives. I worked with several underground newspapers, and chose what I wanted to photograph. A police press pass gave me special access to events.

At peace demonstrations I saw a lot of violence and police brutality. The police almost always provoked the violence, an aspect of the situation the mainstream press was not reporting. Newspaper accounts of demonstrations I had been to bore little relation to the experience I had had, almost as if the reporters had been to a different demonstration.

The establishment media devoted more space to movie stars, corporate announcements, and singular violent crimes than to an expression of social and human conscience by tens of thousands of people.

One night there was a demonstration against South African diamond mines, on Fifth Avenue near Rockefeller Center. The police charged into the peaceful picket line and began hitting people with nightsticks. Everyone ran, but the police caught up with one young man who had a limp and beat him to the ground for no reason whatsoever. I took a picture. Someone yelled that Bobby Kennedy was right

ROBERT KENNEDY, ROCKEFELLER CENTER ICE SKATING RINK, '68

below us in the ice-skating rink.

I ran down and told him that the police were beating people on the street above, naively expecting him to immediately run upstairs and stop it. He was cautious, obviously not wanting or able to get personally involved. I was surprised by his reluctance to get involved. He sent an aide to see what was happening. By that time it was over.

I then rushed my film to the Associated Press, one of the largest press agencies in the world. After the film was processed, the editors saw the picture and told me, "No, it's not for us, we don't want it." That was the first time I had any personal contact with those involved with the news that the world reads, and I saw that they were closed to the truth. It was just as shocking to me as the police brutality I had photographed. The people who controlled the media disliked hippies and were against the demonstrations. Their failure to report events truthfully was not an oversight.

So the pictures were published in the underground press, whose editors sometimes went too far the other way, dehumanizing and condemning anyone who was not on their side — urging anger and aggression rather than peaceful resolution of conflict.

That police brutality was not an isolated incident. I saw it often at other demonstrations.

9

After a while I found the dynamic of many peace demonstrations to be a game between the police and the demonstrators. The question was not who was right or wrong but whether or not you wanted to play that game. You could be the policeman or the demonstrator, but either way you were still part of the fighting. The "isness" of the situation was conflict.

During this time I also took photographs at celebrity press parties because I wanted to be part of the glamorous world which I had seen in media all my life. The famous and would-be-famous went to be seen, publicized, glamorized, and admired. No one was really having fun. It was an ego trip. They painted themselves and made believe they were beautiful, saying in effect, "My breasts are beautiful, my eyebrows are beautiful," but no one said, "My mind is beautiful, my heart is beautiful." It was too artificial for me, and I never felt good about being there. I saw that Hollywood celebrities had no real relationship to my life.

At one awards ceremony Dustin Hoffman told me how ridiculous he thought these events were, and he was obviously uncomfortable about having to be there. We were in a room with chintzy flowered wallpaper, rows of chairs with the actors' names pasted on them, and the actors were lined up like cattle going to slaughter. The absurdity of the star culture with its hero worship, prize awards, and contrived media coverage seemed obvious to us both.

It struck me that when you watch a film

BRITT EKLUND, OPENING NIGHT, NYC, 1968

or a television show, what you see goes inside your head and registers as truth, as reality. This impression goes beyond what you think about it, and becomes part of you, almost like a stamp on your brain. It seemed sad that the whole world was so obsessed with these people because of the illusions created by the films they were in. It was all make-believe, and the truth became visible through my lens.

The photographs that came from these events were often ridiculous, to the point of being humorous. I never meant to take a "bizarre" picture of anyone: they happened by chance and showed me more about what was going on at those parties than I realized while I was there. The camera saw more than I did. It penetrated the illusion of glamour.

I also realized that photographs say just as much about the photographer as they do about the subject. The photos of the press parties exude such an unpleasant atmosphere because I felt out of place at these events. Other photographers, standing next to me, produced traditional, glamorous movie-star images. My pictures reflected that aspect of the events which impacted most on me—the falseness and superficiality. They were a reflection of my inner feelings toward what was happening—a flow of energy, channeled and filtered through my own person. My camera never lied, and taught me much about what I was seeing.

During that time I also discovered the grace of chance. By letting myself be carried along by circumstances at the press parties or peace demonstrations, I would *accidentally* get perfectly composed images—images that were more interesting to me than if I had been able to shoot one which I had visually composed through a decision making process.

Many of my best photographs were made because I had no desire to push aside the people who were standing in front of me. I just held my camera above my head and let myself go with the crowd. From those experiences I learned that chance is one of the most important and useful things in life. I would advise anyone who is serious about photography to try taking pictures without looking through the viewfinder.

With this negative atmosphere prevailing at most peace demonstrations and press parties, I lost interest in photographing them. I had done it. The situations were repetitive, and the pictures began to sour. I wasn't interested in showing violence or people looking strange. I was interested in beauty. I discovered I was an artist, not a violent revolutionary.

PEARL BAILEY, MORT GLANKOFF, *CUE* MAGAZINE AWARDS DINNER, '67

PHOTOS ON PAGES 10 TO 29 WERE TAKEN IN 1967 OR 68 IN NEW YORK CITY UNLESS OTHERWISE NOTED.

WE STAND BESIDE THE MEN WHO HAVE BEEN INDICTED FOR SUPPORT OF DRAFT RESISTANCE. IF THEY ARE SENTENCED, WE, TOO, MUST BE SENTENCED. IF THEY ARE IMPRISONED, WE WILL TAKE THEIR PLACES AND WILL CONTINUE TO USE WHAT MEANS WE CAN TO BRING THIS WAR TO AN END. WE WILL NOT STAND BY SILENTLY AS OUR "GOVERNMENT" CONDUCTS A "CRIMINAL" WAR. WE WILL CONTINUE TO OFFER SUPPORT AS WE HAVE BEEN DOING TO THOSE WHO REFUSE TO SERVE IN VIETNAM AND TO THOSE INDICTED MEN AND ALL OTHERS WHO REFUSE TO BE PASSIVE ACCOMPLICES IN WAR CRIMES. THE WAR IS ILLEGITIMATE AND OUR ACTIONS ARE LEGITIMATE.

In support of Draft Resistance, Rev. William Sloan Coffin (top), Allen Ginsberg (right)

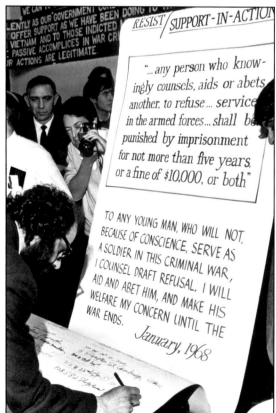

RESIST / SUPPORT-IN-ACTION

"... any person who knowingly counsels, aids or abets another, to refuse ... service in the armed forces ... shall be punished by imprisonment for not more than five years, or a fine of $10,000, or both"

TO ANY YOUNG MAN, WHO WILL NOT, BECAUSE OF CONSCIENCE, SERVE AS A SOLDIER IN THIS CRIMINAL WAR, I COUNSEL DRAFT REFUSAL. I WILL AID AND ABET HIM, AND MAKE HIS WELFARE MY CONCERN UNTIL THE WAR ENDS.

January, 1968

LEGALIZE ABORTION

Abortion Rights demonstration St Patrick's Cathredral

DEMONSTRATION AGAINST SOUTH AFRICAN DIAMOND MINING

PENTAGON PEACE DEMONSTRATION, WASHINGTON, DC, '67

Pro-war demonstrator, Pentagon Peace Demonstration, Washington, DC, '67

PENTAGON PEACE DEMONSTRATION, WASHINGTON, DC, '67

Pro-war demonstrators, Anti-war demonstration, Bryant park,

OPENING NIGHT

We felt that the American culture was more concerned with celebrities than the casualties of the Vietnam War. The absurdity of *Celebrity Culture* often revealed itself to my camera.

Pentagon Peace Demonstration, Washington, DC, 1967

A Demonstrator who was on crutches, was hit by a policeman from behind with a nightstick as police violently broke up a peaceful demonstration against South African diamond mining.

MARLENE DIETRICH, HIDING FROM PHOTOGRAPHERS' FLASHBULBS AT PARTY AFTER PREMIERE OF HER ONE-WOMAN BROADWAY SHOW

MELINA MERCOURI, OPENING NIGHT GALA, NYC, '68

ELIZABETH TAYLOR AND RICHARD BURTON BEING ESCORTED INTO AN OPENING NIGHT GALA

MACY'S THANKSGIVING DAY PARADE

ELECTRONIC NEWS SIGN ON THE NY TIMES BUILDING (WRONGLY) DESCRIBES A PEACE DEMONSTRATION IN THE STREET BELOW, TIMES SQUARE, '67

PEARL BAILEY, CUE MAGAZINE AWARDS PARTY

PEACE DEMONSTRATION, TIMES SQUARE

TOO LATE FOR THE RED CARPET

PEACE DEMONSTRATORS, WASHINGTON SQUARE PARK

PEACE DEMONSTRATION, CENTRAL PARK

PRO-WAR DEMONSTRATORS, ANTI-WAR DEMONSTRATION, BRYANT PARK, NYC

FAYE DUNAWAY, OPENING NIGHT

PEACE DEMONSTRATION, TIMES SQUARE

POLICEMAN HITTING DEMONSTRATOR W. BLACKJACK, PEACE DEOMONSTRATION, WASHINGTON SQUARE PARK

HERMINONE GINGOLD

JOAN COLLINS

ABORTION RIGHTS DEMONSTRATION

High on the Music

The appeal of musicians of the Sixties was that they played from a very deep, very personal, very poetic part of themselves. They tried to express the essence of themselves through their music. Musicians had always tried to express this essence, of course. But in the Sixties they consciously looked for it and went beyond the norms of society to develop a new form of music created as a participatory experience for the audience. They did not simply perform, but interacted with the audience, inviting them to dance, to change their lifestyles, to become part of a large family of like-minded beings. The concert space became a communal space for an evening.

If the Sixties generation wanted to change the world, the musicians were viewed as the leaders. We confused their art with their personalities. As artists they had discovered how to tap into the essence of the time, how to utilize masses of energy to move people and communicate their feelings. In so doing they created a powerful transformative experience for a culture in the midst of an evolutionary elevation of awareness.

But the musicians, so successful at their art, often didn't reach that same level in their personal lives—some failed abysmally—nor were they necessarily gurus in areas other than music. Dylan tried to make this clear to me when we

COUNTRY JOE, ANDERSON THEATER, NYC, '68. MY FIRST LIGHT SHOW CONCERT

met by denying that he was a political leader.

I was never into the personalities of the performers whom I was photographing. When I was shooting a concert, only the music and how the musicians looked as they were playing it mattered. If I didn't like the music, I couldn't take pictures.

Above all, I was into photography for the image. Meaning and content were secondary. This was true even though I wanted to say something with my photos. I felt that the only way to really say something—to create a feeling in the person seeing the photograph—was to present a work of art so well composed that its form touched something within the viewer, helping him or her to open up and understand. Without first opening, a person cannot learn, and so I was a stickler for creative control over my work—especially since, in the beginning, I was not getting paid beyond bare costs for film and paper used to make the prints.

In 1968 two former legitimate Jewish theaters in New York's East Village began presenting psychedelic rock concerts—the Anderson, and Bill Graham's Fillmore East. They were located around the corner from the offices of The Rat, the underground newspaper that I was photographing for. I remember my first concert. Anyone would. It was a new world of fabulous sound, music-filled air, friends everywhere sharing joints, and an incredibly synchronized Joshua Light Show. I was very inspired. It changed my life. I had to take pictures.

The Fillmore East opened in NYC on March 8, 1968. Big Brother and the Holding Company, with Janis Joplin was the headline act. They had just signed with CBS Records. It was a memorable evening.

I had free run of the house because the management of the theater—Bill Graham and John Morris—knew I was working for the underground press. There were very few other photographers, since photographs of rock music were not yet commercially viable. I was able to take pictures from wherever I chose, for as long as I wished, without being worried that an aggressive guard would come along and rip the cameras out of my hands, as began to happen in later years. There was no paranoia, and few restrictions. Today photographers are usually restricted to shooting the first three songs of a concert and are confined to the photographer's pit, directly in front of the stage — which is often not the best place to get a beautiful photograph.

IN THE MC5 COMMUNE, DETROIT, '68

Janis Joplin was one of the few performers I got to know personally while I was photographing in New York City. I got an assignment from New York magazine, to go with Janis and Big Brother to Detroit, where they had a gig at the Grande Ballroom. There we were hosted by John Sinclair and MC-5, the reigning Detroit psychedelic band. Rock bands like Big Brother were part of an underground community which stretched across the nation. We hung out at MC-5's downtown communal apartment, which was big and rambling, with people smoking dope in every room.

I found Janis to be loving, considerate, and lonely. She seemed to experience pain even when she was having pleasure. That she couldn't get as high in real life as she did from her performances saddened and depressed her. Drugs got out of hand. They made the highs higher and the lows lower—too low. Her answer was to do more. She was wrong.

One night, after a big show in New York, I shared a cab with her and a few other members of the band. She directed the cab to drive to the home of a casual friend who she hoped was there. When she got out, she shook her head and with a sad smile said, "Man, what a drag. Here I am a big star and I can't find anyone to be with." We all invited her to stay with us, but she walked away. It was snowing. The cab drove on, taking each of us to our destinations, but for Janis, apparently, there was no place to call home.

PHOTOS ON PAGES 32 TO 83 WERE TAKEN IN 1967 & 1968 IN NEW YORK CITY UNLESS OTHERWISE NOTED.

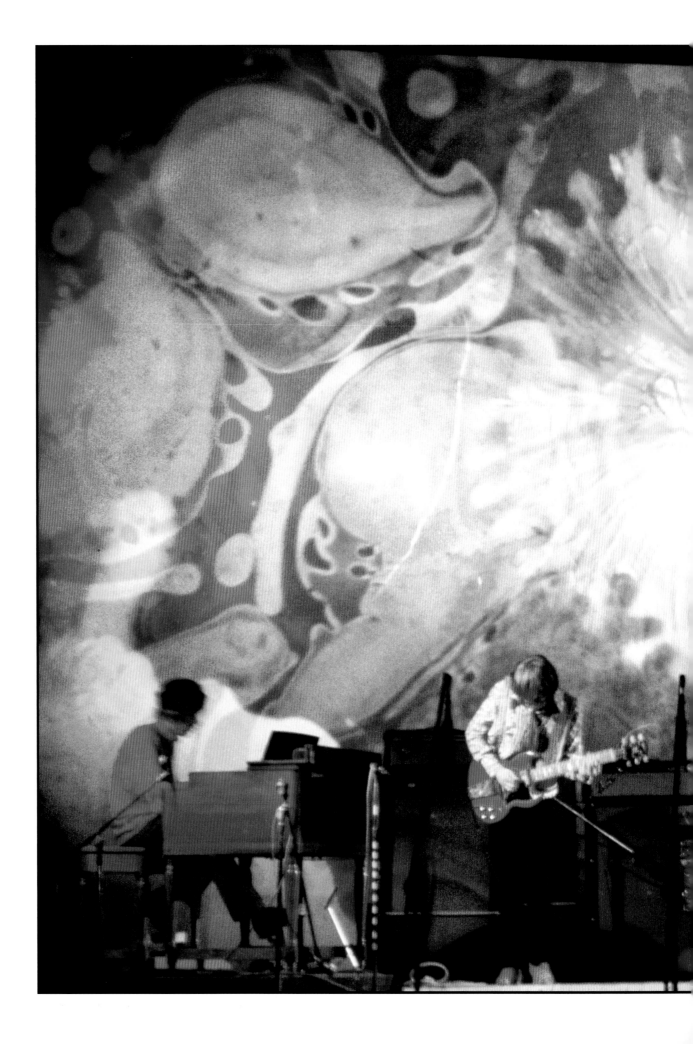

Procol Harem w. Joshua light show, Fillmore East '68

KEITH MOON

JOHN ENTWISTLE, DALTREY

PETE TOWNSHEND

ROGER DALTREY

THE WHO, FILLMORE EAST,
NYC, '68

35

John Lennon, Paul McCartney
Press Conference Announcing the
formation of apple records,
New York City, 1968

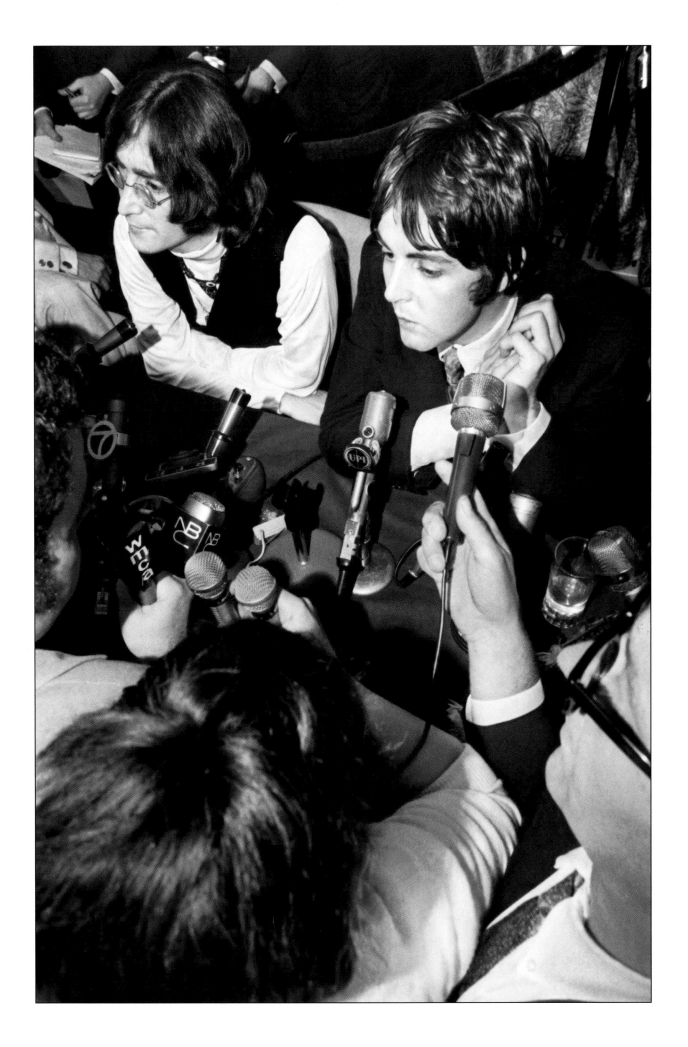

SLY & THE FAMILY STONE, FILLMORE EAST, '68

JEFFERSON AIRPLANE, FILLMORE EAST, '68

THE FUGS, ANDERSON THEATER, NYC, '68

TIM BUCKLEY, FILLMORE EAST, NYC,'68

ALBERT KING, FILLMORE EAST

JOHN LEE HOOKER

CHUCK BERRY, FILLMORE EAST

FRANK ZAPPA, FILLMORE EAST

MELANIE, WHERE SHE GREW UP, THE BRONX

RICHIE HAVENS

TAJ
MAHAL

JOAN
BAEZ

B. B. KING

1968 NEWPORT FOLK FESTIVAL

PETE
SEEGER

Alan Lomax, two unknown, Logan English, Arlo Guthrie, Ramblin' Jack Elliott (w. hat), Oscar Brand, Bess Hawes, Bernice Johnson Reagon, Rev. Frederick Kirkpatrick, Pete Seeger

JOAN BAEZ & MIMI FARINA

RAMBLIN' JACK ELLIOTT

Lee Hays

JOAN BAEZ

1968 NEWPORT FOLK FESTIVAL

BUDDY GUY

DOC WATSON

VAN AND JANET MORRISON, MOONDANCE ALBUM PHOTO SESSION, WOODSTOCK, NY, 1970

ERIC CLAPTON,
DEREK & THE
DOMINOES, PORT
CHESTER, NY, 1970

JIM MORRISON, THE DOORS, HUNTER COLLEGE & THE FILLMORE EAST, NYC, '68

ROBBY KRIEGER, JIM MORRISON, HUNTER COLLEGE, '68

THE JIMI HENDRIX
EXPERIENCE
JOSHUA LIGHT SHOW,
FILLMORE EAST
NYC, '68

JIMI HENDRIX, PRESS
CONFERENCE,
PAN AM BUILDING,
NYC, '68

Jimi Hendrix,
Fillmore East,
NYC, '68

JIMI HENDRIX, FILLMORE EAST, NYC, '68

PIXELATED IMPRESSIONS, HENDRIX AT THE FILLMORE

JIMI HENDRIX,
FILLMORE EAST,
NYC, '68

JIMI HENDRIX, PRESS CONFERENCE, PAN AM BUILDING, NYC, '68

JIMI HENDRIX,
FILLMORE EAST,
NYC, '68

JIMI HENDRIX, FILLMORE EAST, NYC, '68

PRESS CONFERENCE

Janis Joplin

JANIS JOPLIN W. BIG BROTHER DRUMMER DAVE GETZ

JANIS JOPLIN W. BIG BROTHER & THE HOLDING CO., FILLMORE EAST, NYC, '68

JANIS JOPLIN,
ANDERSON THEATER, '68

ALL WITH JOSHUA LIGHT SHOW

PAUL MORRISSEY, ANDY WARHOL, JANIS JOPLIN, TIM BUCKLEY AT MAX'S KANSAS CITY RESTAURANT, NYC, '68

AFTER A GIG, RATNER'S RESTAURANT, NYC, '68

DETROIT AIRPORT, '68

NEWPORT FOLK FESTIVAL, '68

ED SANDERS (THE FUGS), JANIS, ANDERSON THEATER, NYC, '68

ALBERT GROSSMAN, BIG BROTHER & CLIVE DAVIS, PRES. CBS RECORDS.

W. ALBERT GROSSMAN

PRESS PARTY CELEBRATING CBS'S SIGNING OF BIG BROTHER AND THE HOLDING COMPANY

W. ALBERT GROSSMAN

W. CLIVE DAVIS

OPPOSITE PAGE:
TOP: OPENING NIGHT, FILLMORE EAST
BOTTOM: ANDERSON THEATER, NYC, '68

LEANING ON ALBERT'S BACK

W. SAM ANDREW IN GROSSMAN'S OFFICE

GRANDE
BALLROOM,
DETROIT, '68

W. BIG
BROTHER

All taken with Infrared Film for album cover shoots, 1968.

None were selected by the labels.

Ornette Coleman & son, Denardo (top)

Albert Ayler, home & Prospect Park, Brooklyn (Left)

John Lee Hooker, NYC (right).

The Band

One of the first major magazine assignments I got was to photograph Janis Joplin and Big Brother and the Holding Company. They were managed by Albert Grossman, who also managed Bob Dylan. Albert had a distinct dislike for me because of a run-in we had had at a Dylan concert a few months earlier, and he once asked me to leave his office in the middle of a shoot. However, he did allow me some access to his group because the job was for a major magazine.

One night I was photographing Big Brother at a club called Generation, which later became Jimi Hendrix's

NEXT OF KIN

Electric Ladyland Studio. Albert was there, and in between sets, he motioned me into a tiny room in the back of the club. I didn't have a clue what was coming next. He then popped the question—was I "free to take some pictures this weekend in Toronto?" "Of who," I asked. "They don't have a name yet," he replied. I said, "yes."

At the time I didn't know how important that question was. It's funny how some moments stand out in your memory. I can still see the two of us in that tiny room. I had thought he was still mad at me.

Later Myra Friedman, Janis's friend and publicist, told me that Albert had seen the photos of Janis which I had left in her office, and he flipped over them. There was one in particular that showed her hugging him from behind at a press party. He was reaching around behind him while she cuddled up, looking like a little girl; she's kind of goofing a little bit, distracting him while he was doing business. Albert had "liberated" my print and put it on his wall.

It was admirable that Albert was able to forgive me once he recognized my talent. It was also smart. Intuitively he knew that I was the right photographer for the new album—**Music From Big Pink**. He discovered me and gave me my big break. That night he also told me that Dylan might be there for the picture. I felt my life going into high gear.

The first time I heard The Band's music was the night I met Robbie Robertson and Garth Hudson to show them my photographs. After looking at my pictures in the hallway of the recording studio in New York, Robbie brought me into the mixing room where Garth was listening to his masterful organ intro to "Chest Fever" coming full blast from the finest studio speakers.

It was a good beginning. They asked me to meet them in Toronto the following week.

Three of the members of the group picked me up at the airport, and we drove up north to Rick Danko's uncle's farm to take the "next of kin" picture which appeared on the album. This was their way of acknowledging their families, and the importance of their roots to their music. Four of them were from Canada, and Levon Helm was from Arkansas. His parents couldn't make the trip, so we put their picture in the corner of the shot. Dylan didn't come either.

The guys in The Band were different from the other musicians I had been around. Even though they were young, hung out with the best of 'em, and did whatever "irresponsible" things they wanted, there was a deep wisdom and maturity about them. They

IN CANADA

knew about life and about people. You couldn't fool them. They had been around and had seen it all with a really deep comprehension. I liked all of them a lot and felt really comfortable around them—like a kindred soul.

I flew back to New York with John Simon, who had produced the album. When they saw the pictures from Toronto, they liked them, and we made plans to do a shot of the band members alone. On Easter weekend 1968 I went up to photograph them in Woodstock, where they were living in the house they jokingly called Big Pink. Four of them—Levon, Richard Manuel, Garth, and Rick—were living there. Robbie had his own house elsewhere in Woodstock, with his wife, Dominique, a French Canadian journalist.

It was in the basement of this house, that they recorded the basement tapes with Dylan. All the instruments and microphones were set up. Dylan had originally rented the house for them when he brought them to Woodstock.

We took some pictures on Saturday, and I stayed overnight. The next day, Easter Sunday, they were invited to Bob's house, but couldn't bring me with them. I was left at Big Pink with Levon's girlfriend, who wasn't in the mood to go, she said.

We got stoned, and settled in. After a few hours she asked me to drive her somewhere. She wanted to find Levon. So we drove through winding wooded roads, up a mountain, and pulled off the road in front of a big old brown wooden house. As we were walking inside, she told me, "This is Bob's house."

Sara Dylan greeted us at the door, her inner warmth matching her physical beauty. She didn't know exactly who I was, but immediately made me feel welcome, offered me a drink, and invited me to be comfortable, which I definitely was not. In retrospect I think that her energy—who she was—was responsible for Bob's choosing a positive path at that point in his life.

I looked around the large living room: vaulted ceiling, dark wooden beams, picture window looking out over the trees, a big fireplace, and a grand piano in the corner. I saw a couple of the Band members there, and felt uneasy since they had not asked me to come.

After what now seems like less than a minute, Levon's girlfriend was back and wanted to leave. She hadn't found him and wanted to look further. So we left. I don't even know if I saw Bob or not. It was all too fast, but that was the first time I might have met him.

We drove down through some more winding Woodstock country roads and pulled up to another house. She knew the woman who lived there and suspected that Levon was 'visiting.' We parked the car, got out, and walked up to the house. There were several doors, and she went over to one on the other side, while I waited by the car. After a moment, Levon peeked out of another door, and asked me what was going on. I told him, and he told me to make believe I hadn't seen him. His girlfriend came back a minute later, having gotten no answer, and we left. I didn't say anything, and we drove back to Big Pink. It was quite a ride.

We took several beautiful photographs at Big Pink. One was a picture of

In front of Big Pink, West Saugerties, NY, Easter Sunday '68

them taken from behind, sitting on a bench in front of a pond. They had explained that they didn't want a name because they wanted the focus to be on the music, not on themselves., and didn't want to be "labeled" and defined by the audience's preconceptions. They wanted to be free to change musically. So they wanted to stay almost anonymous, which I think we captured in that photograph.

But they didn't feel it was right, I don't know why. So I went back to do a second shoot. We did some nice shots at a few different places, but those weren't what they wanted either. But they decided to stick with me and try a third time. We had a real nice personal connection.

We talked about what was missing in the photos, and I showed them a book of photographs of the Old West and suggested we go for that look. They liked the idea.

I realized that the subjects of those photographs were very connected to the land, they seemed to be planted there. We looked around for the right place to take the shot and found it in their front yard.

The other element present in the old photographs was respect. People took the camera seriously. A photographer's visit was an important and unusual occasion. People stood up straight and looked right at the camera, which made them look dignified. People were a different sort in those days. They were connected to the earth, there were no modern conveniences. Of course, I couldn't have created that old-time classic look with just anyone. It was their spirits that came out and greeted the opportunity for self-expression.

I spent a lot of time in Woodstock, photographing, showing them the pictures, and just hanging out. They showed me the country life, and introduced me to their friends. I loved it. I went to Los Angeles to photograph them for their second album, **The Band**, which they were recording in Los Angeles, and for their debut performance at the Fillmore West in San Francisco.

They didn't ask me to do their third album, but by that time I wasn't interested in music photography anymore. I had done it and had embraced a different, more personal, creative direction—photographing the love I was experiencing everyday with my wife and new baby.

86

BIG PINK
ALBUM SHOOT

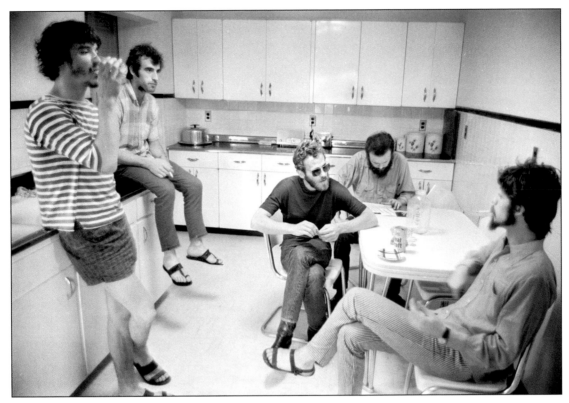

Big Pink

RICK DANKO, '68

LEVON & ROBBIE, LEVON & RICHARD'S HOUSE, WOODSTOCK, '68. THE **BIG PINK** ALBUM PHOTO WAS TAKEN RIGHT OUTSIDE THIS WINDOW.

MUSIC FROM
BIG PINK
ALBUM PHOTO

LEVON HELM, FILLMORE EAST, NYC, '69

ROBBIE & DOMINIQUE ROBERTSON, FILLMORE EAST, '69

RICHARD MANUEL, AT HOME, 1968

BASEMENT OF RICK'S HOUSE, '69

RECORDING *THE BAND* ALBUM, L.A., '69

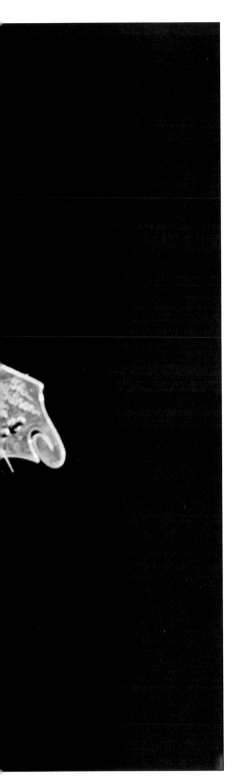

Robbie and Levon, upstairs at Rick's house, '69

Levon Helm, Fillmore West, S.F., '69

Rick Danko w. Hamlet

Photos on following four pages taken for **The Band** album, Woodstock, 1969

The Band
album cover photo
(L to R)
Richard Manuel
Levon Helm
Rick Danko
Garth Hudson
Robbie Robertson

Infrared Film
(clockwise)
Rick, Richard
Levon, Robbie

Photographing Bob Dylan

The first time I photographed Dylan was at the Woody Guthrie Memorial Concert at Carnegie Hall in New York City in 1967. It was his first public appearance since his motorcycle accident a year earlier. He was playing with The Band, who were unknown at that time.

I was just starting my photographic career and wanted to see the show as well as take some pictures that I could sell. So I called up Dylan's office, identified myself as a photographer for an underground newspaper, and asked for two press tickets. I brought my cameras to the concert, assuming that since they'd given me

LEVON HELM, RICK DANKO, DYLAN, ROBBIE ROBERTSON, WOODY GUTHRIE MEMORIAL CONCERT, '67

tickets as a photographer, I could take photographs. But when I got to Carnegie Hall, there were signs posted stating "No Photographs Allowed," and the ushers insisted that I check my cameras. I argued, showing my press pass and the tickets from Dylan's office, but to no avail. So I said, "OK, no pictures allowed," and checked half my cameras, but kept the other half—everything that would fit into my pockets and my date's bag.

I had a good seat near the front of the hall. Dylan came on stage, and I started snapping away, clicking my shutter only during the loud passages in order to be as discreet as possible.

After a couple of songs Arlene Cunningham, who worked for Dylan's manager, Albert Grossman, spotted me taking photographs. Soon she and Albert, whom I did not know at the time, and a guard were all waving to me from the side of the hall telling me to stop taking photographs. I pretended not to see their increasingly frantic waving.

Then Albert gestured to the guard to get me out of the seat. Meanwhile Dylan was playing with The Band, and it was very exciting. The guard came toward me. I knew what was going to happen next. They always go for your film.

So I rewound the film I had shot and gave it to my lady friend, with instructions not to give it up under any circumstances. I quickly put another roll of film into the camera. I didn't want to create a scene and disrupt the concert, so we

108

followed the guard out into the posh, carpeted, chandeliered lobby where Albert, Arlene, and a few other people quickly surrounded us.

Albert demanded the film, and I adamantly refused, acting as if it were gold. "There's no way I'm gonna give you this film." But Arlene had seen me switch and was trying to tell him, but he was too engrossed in the mock battle I was staging. Every time I heard Arlene say, "She's got the film!", I raised my voice a bit, repeating, "You're not gonna get this film! You have no right to do this," and so on. I really carried on—I wasn't violent or nasty, just loud, to distract him from her.

While I argued with him, I held the camera in front of me, presenting it to him without being obvious about it, knowing he would grab it. Finally he did and ripped the film out, exposing it and making it even blanker, I guess. After that we left, with the film safely hidden away. It never bothered me that I missed the rest of the concert. Only the film mattered. That was the first time I saw Bob Dylan, and the last time I saw my lady friend.

Despite that first strange encounter with Albert, my life brought me to Dylan again. My first record-album assignment was **Music From Big Pink**, which had a painting by Dylan on the cover. I knew that everyone would read the credits to see his name and would then read my name next to his. That was when I realized that I was going to be well known. I was surprised.

Curiously, because our names are anagrams of each other—DYLAN/LANDY—many people thought I didn't exist—that he was me under an alias! There have even been articles about it.

OUTSIDE HIS BYRDCLIFFE HOUSE

Everyone liked the Big Pink photographs, and shortly afterward Al Aronowitz, a writer and friend of Dylan's, asked me to photograph Bob for the cover of **The Saturday Evening Post**.

I rented a little VW bug and drove up from the city to the center of Woodstock, where Al was waiting and led me the rest of the way through the winding country roads. We pulled into Bob's driveway and Al went inside to tell Bob we were here. I waited. This was during the height of his fame, when he had only been seen publicly once in a couple of years, and many people thought he had died in a motorcycle accident.

Aronowitz emerged from the house with Bob following him. He introduced us, jumpd in his car and sped off, leaving me alone with this mysterious person. Bob told me how much he liked the Band photos, grabbed his guitar, sat on an old tire, and began playing while I took pictures. It occurred to me that millions of people would be thrilled to be ten feet away from Bob Dylan while he was playing, but he was so casual, it seemed normal to me. He suggested some other things. "This is what I do up here, take a picture," he said while putting the garbage cans away. He sat on the step of his equipment van and then in front of an old British cab he owned. After a while he asked to use the camera. For some of the pictures I used infrared color film, which made the leaves bright red.

Although he was comfortable with me, he was nervous in front of the camera, and his uneasiness made it difficult for me. I was never the kind of photographer who talked people into feeling good. I let them *be* the way they were and photographed it. Usually it worked out. Because

I flowed with whatever mood they were in, without resistance, things usually lightened up.

He asked me to come back with the pictures when they were ready, which I did the following week. He liked the photos, and we started to hang out a bit. He suggested that I take photographs of him with Sara and the children. I don't think he had ever asked anyone else to do that. It seemed natural to me, and I was thrilled to photograph them because I thought they were a beautiful family. The value of the photos never entered my mind. I was immersed in the wonderful energy they had and felt joyous to document it. For many years afterward I resisted selling them, even though I was often in dire financial straits when I lived in Europe.

He was very happy, in love with his lovely and gracious wife, Sara, and with his family. He was hiding from the world, savoring the magical experience of having young

SHOOTING THE PHOTOGRAPHER, W. JESSE

children. That's why I didn't publish the pictures for many years. He cherished his privacy and didn't want any media attention on his family.

I was very impressed with Bob. He was a very special person. He intuitively understood what was going on in a situation. There was a feeling you got when you were with him that was exciting. I believe it was the flow of creative energy surrounding him that sort of spilled over onto you. Over the years I've seen him walk into rooms, even in the presence of other very famous people, and suddenly everyone's attention becomes totally focused on him. It's difficult to have this type of charisma: people always want a piece of you.

I remember admiring the way he dealt with his five-year-old son, Jesse, who was whining in frustration wanting Bob to help him move a toy car. I would have gone over and done it for him, but Bob encouraged him, "C'mon, Jesse, you can do it, just keep trying." And Jesse, with a big smile of satisfaction, did it. I was very impressed by Bob's instinct to teach him self-reliance.

We got pretty friendly, and I stayed overnight in his home three or four times. We talked about different things. When I asked him about politics, he told me he wasn't very interested in politics and didn't know much about it. I was shocked because his music was considered to be the Magna Carta of radical Sixties political thought. I asked him how he wrote those songs if he didn't know anything, and he said that he didn't create those ideas but simply "picked up what was in the air, and gave it back to people in another form." My interpretation is that he intuited the future of political thought and turned it into music—kind of like a seer singing poetry. His skill, he acknowledged, was "knowing how to use the language." Although he disclaimed having any interest in the political process, I felt he was interested in social justice.

About a year later, during another conversation at his house, he expressed some fairly conservative political views, which really surprised me. I couldn't believe it, but he seemed serious. However, while driving home, I ran into Richard Manuel of The Band, by chance. I told Richard what Bob had just said. Richard chuckled and told me Bob could have been putting me on, that he liked to put people on just to confuse them. I had observed that Bob liked to be mysterious because he felt it encouraged people to think for themselves. One of Bob's major themes was that people shouldn't blindly follow or accept things.

So I never repeated what Bob told me, but I still wonder.

Another aspect of Dylan which impressed me was that he listened more than he talked. He brought someone out rather than talking about what he already knew. From seeing him do this, I understood that silence could be wiser than words.

I think this time in Woodstock was a transformative period for him. He was learning to feel and express love through his family experience. His music from this period reflects that: It's light, homey and havenlike. He was no longer heavy-handed. Woodstock is a very special place; the feeling in the air is wonderful. It has a history of spirituality going back to the Native Americans. The Tibetan Buddhists have established a center there because they feel it is on one of the main energy meridians in North America.

ELLIOTT LANDY BY BOB DYLAN

Just after **The Saturday Evening Post** shoot I moved to Woodstock. I had fallen in love with the lifestyle there and expected that I would do more work with Dylan and the Band. I used to see Bob occasionally here and there. One night I bumped into him and Sara as they were driving up to the Grand Union. He asked if I would mind going in and getting a few cans of cat food; they had just run out.

In early 1969 he called and asked me to take a picture for the back of his new album, *Nashville Skyline*. He had the front cover already picked out—a picture of the skyline of Nashville, where he had recorded the album.

We didn't know what to do; we had no concepts when we started. We met, and he suggested that we take a picture in front of the bakery in Woodstock with his son, Jesse, and two local Woodstock people. The brown leather jacket he was wearing was the same one he had worn for the covers of *John Wesley Harding* and *Blonde on Blonde*.

He was still uncomfortable being photographed, and therefore I was uncomfortable photographing him, but we stayed with it. We took some pictures at the bakery and then went to my house and hung out.

I projected some slides, nudes I had just taken of a young woman, and he started to laugh. I asked him what was funny, and he said, "Don't you see the story?" "What story?" "Run them again."

As the pictures were projected, he wrote some captions and read them to me. They parlayed the expressions on the woman's face into an absurdly funny dialogue. He wrote quickly for a while, throwing some pages away, perfecting the story which we both thought was incredibly funny. He said we should publish them.

A little while later he left but came back in a few minutes and retrieved his discarded notes from the wastebasket. I wouldn't have thought to keep them, but I'm sure he had had some bad experiences.

I mentioned the project to him several times after that but he said he couldn't find the notes. Over the years the photographs have disappeared as well.

That same day we took some photographs outside my house. He had his glasses on, but there wasn't any discussion about "I don't want to have the glasses on the album" or anything like that. We were just easy. It was very casual. He wanted some pictures, we took them, and neither of us conceptualized it. I'm spontaneous when I work, and so is he. An art director might have said, "Take the glasses off," but neither he nor I thought about it. However people present themselves is how I photograph them—I don't judge it.

Then on another afternoon I went over to his place. As we left the house, he grabbed a hat, and asked, "Do you think we could use this?" I had no idea if it would be good or not, so I told him "take it, and we'll see." We walked around through the woods behind his house looking for a good spot. It had just been raining, we had boots on, and he was carrying this hat.

He paused for a moment, apparently inspired, and said, "What about taking one from down there?" pointing to the ground. As I started kneeling, I saw that it was muddy but kept going. "Do you think I should wear this?" he asked, starting to put on his hat, smiling because it was kind of a goof, and he was having fun visualizing himself in this silly-looking traditional hat. "I don't know," I said as I snapped the shutter. It all happened so fast. If I had had any resistance in me, I would have missed the photograph that became the cover of *Nashville Skyline*. It is best to be open to life.

During those days in Woodstock he was really open and in a good mood. It was sunny out and we just followed our instincts. It was the first picture of him smiling, and in my opinion reflects the inner spirit, the loving essence of the man behind all the inspiring music he has given us. Someone told me that the reason people like it so much is that it makes them happy.

Every review of the album mentioned his smile on the cover. No one talked about the photograph itself. For me that is requisite for a "good" photograph. The medium itself should be invisible. It shouldn't make you look at it and think, "What a great photograph this is," but rather should make you focus on what is in the photograph: "Look at that child, look at the flower, look at that person, how fantastic."

Nearly everyone of my generation knows the photograph, and many have acknowledged it as an image that has had great meaning to them. Perhaps it reflects the love we were all seeking to find through making the world a better place.

And so this was a magical picture for all of us. It certainly assured my reputation as a photographer. My bill for the shoot, which in addition to my fee, included an array of items such as gas, tolls, film, etc., came to exactly $777. In metaphysics 777 is the number of mystical manifestation, the magical number, representing mysteries, the occult, clairvoyance, magic, the seven principles of man, the universe, and also the notes on a musical scale. I was awed by this incredible coincidence. It strengthened my feeling that everything is interconnected in ways which the logical mind cannot explain: We are all one.

I brought the picture to CBS Records and told them that Dylan didn't want any writing on the cover, no names, logos, or other sales tools. This was Bob's way of saying that his music was not created as a commercial pursuit. Despite his wishes, CBS put their logo in the upper left-hand corner, and although small and seemingly insignificant, this ruins the three-dimensionality of the image. While looking at the record, cover the logo, then uncover and cover it again. It will appear to go from two to three dimensions and back.

The following summer, in 1970, he called and asked me if I would photograph some of his drawings. He had started painting in Woodstock some years before. I thought his work was very beautiful. His drawings reminded me of Van Gogh's. Looking back at it now, I find this similarity interesting, as Van Gogh was obsessive about the purity and spirituality of his painting, while Dylan is the same about the purity of his music, treating it with reverence, to be given in pure form to the people, not adulterated by commercial interests. This is why he has never sold any of his songs for commercials, one of the few artists to maintain that purity of purpose which the planet needs to survive.

A few weeks later Al Aronowitz called from Bob's and asked me to come over to help set up a large trampoline. Bob had moved into a newer, brighter, and more spacious house. We set up the trampoline, and Bob asked me to take some pictures of the kids and then some of him doing some funny stuff. It was a great day.

In the fall both he and I moved to Manhattan. One time, hidden under a knit cap and dark glasses, he came over to my loft.

It was a different Dylan than I had known in Woodstock. He invited us (my wife and year old daughter, Joiwind) to a birthday party at his MacDougal Street home. We went, had a fun day, and said we'd see each other again soon, but shortly after that he went to Mexico to make a film, and I left for Europe, where I stayed for seven years.

In 1978, when I returned from Europe, I went to a concert but wasn't allowed to see him. After the concert, by chance, I met him in the elevator backstage as he was going to the venue reception. He said hello but didn't invite me along when he got out. Since then we've spoken occasionally but our connection has never been renewed and I'm sorry for the lost opportunity to do creative work. Bob was always suggesting that we put pictures and words together, but somehow the projects never happened.

SHREDNI VOLPER, LEVON HELM, DYLAN, RICK DANKO, LONE STAR CAFE, NYC, '83

BYRDCLIFF HOUSE, '68

W. JESSE AND MARIA, BYRDCLIFFE, '68

w. Sara & Jesse, Byrdcliffe, '68

w. Jesse, Byrdcliffe home, '68

OUTSIDE MY HOUSE, WOODSTOCK, '69

WITH DEAN, DAVID & JESSE, WOODSTOCK TOWN SQUARE, '69

ON THE TRAMPOLINE, OHAYO MTN. RD. HOME, WOODSTOCK, '69

W. SAM AND ANNA, 1970

OHAYO MOUNTAIN RD. HOME, WOODSTOCK, '69

"TAKE ONE OF
ME LIKE THIS."
1970

This photo has become my most popular image of Bob. In addition to its visual beauty, I feel it sub-consciously communicates the otherworldliness of his musical vision—a place he reached to get the words and music which transformed so many of us.

Taken with Kodak Infrared film which is sensitive to both visible and infrared light, using a yellow filter, the green trees of summer were transformed into red, giving the photograph a surrealistic look and feel. At the time, neither Bob nor I realized how special it was.

INTRODUCTION BY
JERRY GARCIA

The thing about Woodstock was that you could feel the presence of invisible time travelers from the future who had come back to see it. You could sense the significance of the event as it was happening. There was a kind of swollen historicity—a truly pregnant moment. You definitely knew that this was a milestone, it was in the air.

As a human being I had a wonderful time, hanging out with friends in the music business and sharing great little jams. But our performance onstage—the Dead's part in Woodstock— was musically a total disaster that is best left forgotten. I've certainly been trying to forget it for 25 years.

Yet other musicians had their careers explode there. It was truly a special moment, which you can still hear and see.

—JERRY GARCIA

WOODSTOCK
An Aquarian Exposition

3 Days of Peace & Music
August 15, 16, 17, 1969 – Bethel, New York

In the summer of 1969, Mike Lang rode his motorcycle over to my house in Woodstock and asked if I would be interested in photographing a festival he was planning. It was one of the most important *yeses* I ever said. We didn't talk about money except to say that we would work it out. It wasn't even a handshake—it was preordained.

On August 15, 16, and 17, 1969, nearly 500,000 people gathered together to celebrate life. They came looking for music and new ways. They found a hard path—there were miles to walk; rain and mud; not much food to eat, nor shelter to sleep beneath; life was not as they usually knew it.

But something happened. There was peace and harmony despite conditions that might have set off riots. Most everyone lived in consideration and enjoyment with everyone else. Woodstock became a symbol to the world of a better way of life—of freedom, of love, of spiritual union between many. There was hope.

Years have passed. "What has happened...where has Woodstock gone?" Words are heard: "It was a fluke." "It can never happen again." "It was not real."

The coming of a new consciousness is a slow process. Woodstock is a way of thinking, a way of being—kindness, consideration, sharing and enjoying; life as it should be and would be if we lived that way.

Astrologically, the birth of the age of Aquarius is upon us—an age of peace and understanding, a golden age. Like all births, the birth of this new consciousness is difficult. Old ways are falling as new ways evolve. The time of labor nears. A soft seedling must break

through a hard seed shell. A baby comes through a birth which can be painful.

Change is often difficult, but what is outside the new door is usually better than what was behind the old. We are given habits by the culture we grow in, the physical realities of our planet, and the needs we have. With the coming of new, clean technologies, physical wants can be met — people no longer have to fight to survive. There can be enough for everyone.

Woodstock showed us that people can live together in a peaceful and sharing way. It showed that the goal many were going toward during those years was reachable. It actually happened for 500,000 people at one time for three days.

The mystical teachings tell us that with the birth of each age there is a sign, a teacher, which appears to lead the way. As Christ was the example for a world 2,000 years ago, so the experience at Woodstock can be an example for our world today. Just as the birth of Jesus could find no place, so, too, Woodstock was without welcome—yet both found their destined place to be—one in Bethlehem, the other in Bethel; the similarity of names whispering to us of a cosmic declaration, an intelligence beyond our own, telling us that our ideals could be made real, that a new time was approaching— telling us to keep on trying.

Twenty-five years ago, in the age of accidents, in the time of free-flowing thought, unbridled energy, and expanding love, a curly-headed kid persuaded a group of supposedly sane people that it would be fun to put together thirty bands, sixty Hog Farmers, twenty-five Indians, and three hundred workers in a field in upstate New York and have a festival and invite the world—who came.

For three days and three nights Chris, Mel, Stan, Lee, Joel, Penny, John, Chip, Wavy, and many, many others kept the water running, the food arriving, the communications functioning, the medical tents supplied, and the music flowing.

For three days and three nights the hundreds of thousands that flooded Max's farm hills shared, laughed, got wet, shared some more, listened, napped, ate, talked, sang, and shared some more, and with not one act of physical violence showed the world what a generation was made of, what peace, love, and music were really all about.

It was fun, it was magic. It was also understood that it was important, it was a risk, it was unique. It was entertainment at its best.

It was responsibility with flowers in its hair. It was the garden, it was Woodstock. It was something every face in this book carries in his or her heart and is proud of.

—JOHN MORRIS

138

SRI SWAMI SATCHIDANANDA
EXCERPTS FROM HIS OPENING ADDRESS TO THE FESTIVAL AUDIENCE

Through music, we can work wonders. Music is a celestial sound and it is the sound that controls the whole universe, not the atomic vibrations.

Sound energy, sound power, is much, much greater than any other power in this world. Through that sacred art of music, let us find peace that will pervade all over the globe.

Often we hear groups of people shouting, "Fight for Peace." I still don't understand how they are going to fight and then find peace. Therefore, let us not fight for peace but let us find peace within ourselves first.

The future of the whole world is in your hands. You can make or break it. But, you are really here to make the world and not to break it. I am seeing it. There is a dynamic manpower here. The hearts are meeting. The entire world is going to watch this and know what American youth can do for humanity.

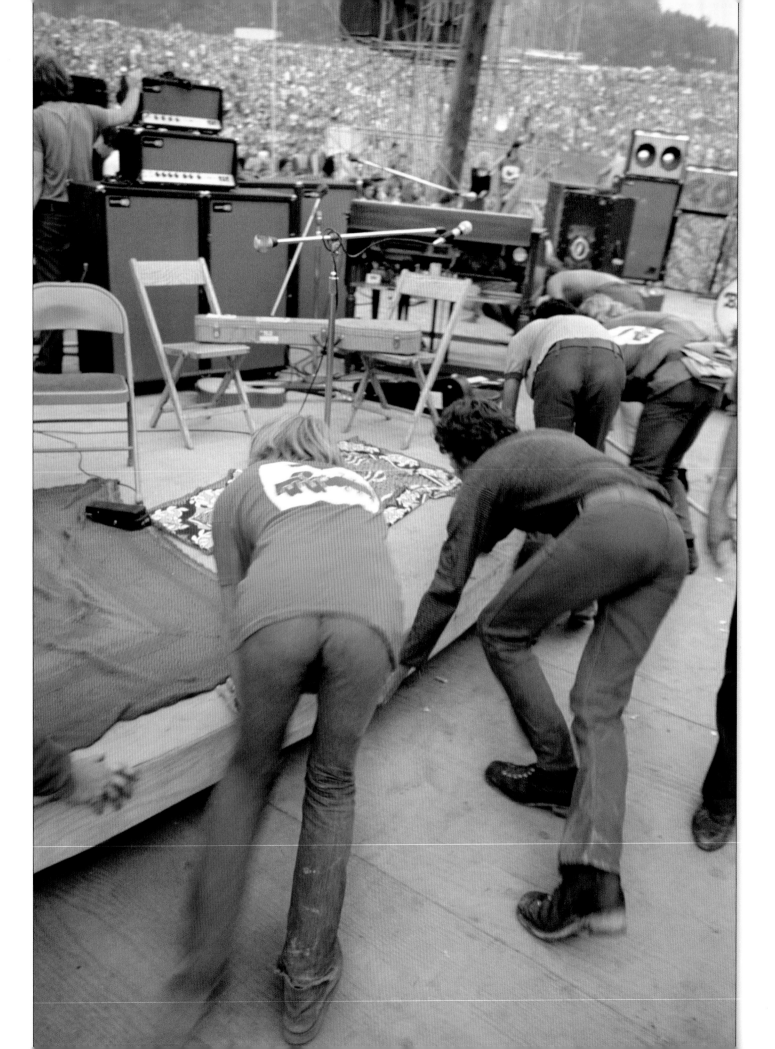

JOHN MORRIS
PRODUCTION COORDINATOR,
STAGE ANNOUNCER, PICKED THE BANDS

I had run Filmore East for Bill Graham, so I knew most of the agents. The Who had turned us down. Frank Barcelone, who is the president of Premiere Talent, was and is one of the major rock-and-roll agents. He has U2 and Springstein, and in those days he had the Who and Steve Winwood.

We had Pete Townshend to dinner at Frank's apartment. We fed him, started pouring wine into him, and talked about Woodstock. Peter kept saying, "No, we don't want to." We kept pouring brandy into him on top of the wine, and about five o'clock in the morning Peter was sitting in the corner all scrunched up saying, "All right. I'll play the thing. Can I go to sleep? Please?"

David Bird, the hot poster designer of that period, did a very art-nouveau, beautiful, very elaborate poster. It was printed, but it just wasn't right. Arnie Skolnick, who did the poster in the end, had a four-year-old-daughter who was playing with construction materials and little blunt scissors, cutting things out. Arnie couldn't come up with an idea when suddenly he went, "Oh." He picked up her paper and scissors, cut out the bird and the arm of the guitar, walked in the next day, and said, "Here." We said, "Wow," and that was the poster. Total accident.

We had about four hundred people working at the site who had just shown up to help. Chris Langhart, our technical director would say, "Okay, who's a carpenter?" and whoever held up their hands, they were carpenters for a day. "Who's a plumber?" And when the guy who said he was a carpenter smashed his thumb or the plumber taped himself to the pipe, Langhart would shift him over to another crew, and that was how Langhart handled the labor. We never advertised for helpers.

JOHN MORRIS, MORNING, BACKSTAGE

Al Aronowitz, a columnist for the New York Post, followed Langhart from making his early-morning cattle call, with "Who's a carpenter? Who's a plumber?" to digging holes, putting in wells, distributing pipes, getting telephone lines in, and he wrote this article that appeared on the first day of Woodstock. As I read it, the first thing I saw was this typo, "I spent the day yesterday with the technical man, 'Christ' Langhart." It was a miracle because 'Chris' finally got the credit he deserved. People don't write about the guys who build things and make it all happen.

The rain made it miserable. It wasn't even worth wearing raincoats or boots. It was warm and humid. It made the construction insane. People were working in mud up to their knees, building roads, putting in telephone lines. Everything was soaking wet, so everything got slowed to death.

The largest single concert anybody had had before Woodstock was the Beatles at Shea Stadium, which was fifty-five thousand people. Monterey, which had been a year or two before, was thirty-five thousand people over three days. The first words said at Woodstock publicly over the P.A. were me saying, "Holy shit," and about six hundred thousand people laughed. I can remember feeling a very heavy responsibility, realizing that what you say is going to have a very strong influence on the crowd getting along, having a good time, going through all the rainstorms, the heat, and cooperating with one another. And we had some very good people like Wavy saying, "We're going to make breakfast in bed for six hundred thousand people."

During the planning I went down to Santa Fe, New Mexico, to an Indian school and brought twenty-five American Indian kids to Woodstock. They came up with the Hog Farm on the plane. They were part of the arts fair, but they never got to show their art. Instead they ended up showing people how to build campfires.

The Hog Farm was brought in to set up a camping area. They became our security because the cops were pulled off by the police commissioner in New York, although a bunch of them did come up anyway. The Hog Farm was there to organize East Coast kids who were not used to camping. These kids showed up with penny loafers and a can of beans in a paper bag and forgot to bring a can opener. The Hog Farm ran a commune down in the Southwest and had organized major events.

Lisa Law, who was one of them, was the only woman that I've ever dealt with in my life who thoroughly terrorized me. She came into my office in my trailer and said, "Give me three thousand dollars to feed people. If you don't give it to me, they're going to starve." And this was three days before the festival. She does this whole number, I mean literally, putting me up against the wall, with "I gotta have this, that"...and I thought three thousand dollars is cheap to get rid of this woman. I wrote a check and handed it to her, and she proceeded to go straight to New York to do exactly the same thing to John Roberts, get another three thousand dollars, and go buy five hundred pounds of bulgur wheat and three hundred pounds of rice. She probably fed a quarter of a million people during the festival who didn't have money to buy concession things. They just set up this gigantic kitchen that operated twenty-four hours a day throughout the whole festival, and she did exactly what she said she was going to do. Lisa is a friend to this day. She keeps saying to me, "How come you're not scared of me anymore?"

It became a free festival because everybody was already in before the fences were completed. All of a sudden the field was entirely full of people. There was a conference immediately. Artie Kornfeld suggested that we have collection baskets in the audience. I threw my hands in the air like, "Oh, now I've heard everything." I called John Roberts and Joel Rosenman in the White Lake office, and they agreed there was no way to move vast numbers of people out of that field. John was making a major decision, he was kissing a couple of million dollars good-bye. A pretty heavy decision for

a twenty-six-year-old. He was an absolute gentleman at all times. After the festival he made sure that absolutely everybody got paid. I have a lot of respect for him.

We had planned this concert that we thought was going to draw seventy-five thousand people. In fact I had a bet with Michael Lang, which he has never asked me to pay, that I would give him one hundred dollars for every thousand people over seventy-five thousand. I never added up—and thank goodness Michael's never added up—how much I would have owed him, but suddenly there were six hundred thousand people in the field and another million and a half trying to get in. We're hiring helicopters, getting water, very different from a laid-back concert. We were suddenly in the city-management business dealing with serious risk to life and limb.

The governor of the state of New York had decided he was going to send in the National Guard and send all these people home. So I spent the first part of Friday arguing with Rockefeller's people. Thank God I was able to prevent what would have become Attica.

One of the nicer things was when the state police said that during the festival there was not one case of physical violence. What almost broke that was this group called Tom Newman and the Crazies, from the Lower East Side. We got word that they were going to burn down the concession stands because "food should be free." Someone went on stage—myself or Abbie Hoffman, who was there with the Yippies—and asked people to get around the concession stands and make sure that nobody caused any trouble. These guys came. They had bandanas over their heads. They were Maoists at that time—you know, they had read the book—and they came charging out and literally got smothered by about thirty to forty thousand people, who said, "Hey, man, cool it, I mean they're not great hot dogs, but they're the hot dogs we have." And, boom. It just calmed down with no physical violence whatsoever.

Richie Havens was the first act because we suddenly realized that we did not have any way to get artists from their hotels. The state police have a satellite photograph showing an immediate twenty-mile area and seventeen miles in a circle around that site blocked solid. That's why we got the helicopters, because we figured it was the only way to get people in. I literally turned around to Annie, my then-wife, and said, "Look up 'Helicopter' in the Yellow Pages and hire every single one." I grabbed Richie and said, "I know you're not supposed to be on until third or whatever, but you're here." He played three encores and didn't know what else to sing so he started strumming and singing about what was in front of him—"Freedom." That's how the song got created.

It was an accident that Swami Satchidananda came saying that he would like to speak to the audience and I thought 'so why not? I haven't got any acts. Let's put him on with all his followers sitting around him.' He talked about peace and leveled everything out. We surmounted thing after thing because there was such goodwill.

Friday night was sort of peaceful and calm. Everybody curled up and covered themselves. Baez, appearing last, sang "Ave Maria" and some of her greats. Her wonderful voice put everybody to sleep.

We got drizzle on Saturday—it was okay—can we have some sun, please? And on Sunday it was fabulous. Then we got a thunderstorm with winds that were over fifty-five miles per hour. Twenty minutes before, I was trying to see if we could get fire trucks in to spray the crowd because it was so hot. All this moisture was coming up from the ground and we were starting to get heat-prostration problems and then, thank you, we didn't need the fire engines. The great thing was, Cocker was singing and it made it feel like he had rustled it up.

Most of the medical problems were cut feet, heat or sunburn. But we lost three people, I believe. One kid who put his sleeping bag down between a trailer and a tractor was run over accidentally in the middle of the night and two other guys died in hospitals. One was a Marine who had come out of Vietnam, had some kind of malarial disease and was misdiagnosed as being a heroin overdose. The other had a burst appendix. We did ask Rockefeller's people for more medical facilities. I was on stage and it looked like the opening of Apocalypse Now with a formation of Hueys flying in; and I'm saying, 'Uh-oh, when the audience sees this, they are going to be really upset, and we've got a problem.' Then I saw the red crosses and said, "Ladies and gentlemen, the United States Army Medical Corps has come to help us." The roar of the crowd almost knocked the helicopters out of the air. It went from something that could have been really nasty to something that became totally positive. And they were a big help, they were great.

During the bad thunderstorm I almost had a nervous breakdown. The scaffolding towers, which weighed five hundred to six hundred pounds apiece, were swaying. Our immediate concern was to get people away from them. We had thunder, lightning, and rain. Armageddon was on my mind. Somebody had just said to me that Joan Baez was having a miscarriage. My dog was lost. My then-wife, Annie, had fallen and broken her ankle, and somebody said there was a guy in the audience with a gun. I had to keep the mike and therefore the electricity on because it was the only way to communicate with people. The mike was shorting out and I'm saying, "Move away from the towers. It will be okay. Everybody just hang on. We're going to ride this through. We've been through everything else." We offered them breakfast in bed; we told them the acts were going to be on; we had a symbiotic relationship at that point and you couldn't walk out on them.

Then there were the scheduling screw-ups. Sha Na Na was shoved around and went on at dawn. And Eddie Goodgold, one of the nicer people on the face of the earth, was going bananas. He was their manager, and I just kept saying, "Ed, hang in there, it will work out." Sha Na Na lived another twenty years because of their performance at Woodstock.

Bill Belmont came to me and said, "Sly is not ready to go on. Sly doesn't feel the vibes." Well, at this point I didn't feel the vibes either. He was doing a star act. It wasn't a matter of being begged, he'd been begged. I looked at Belmont and we both said, "Do a Bill Graham." I grabbed Sly and lifted him up in the air, and said, "If you're not on stage in three minutes, I'm going to take your head off," He just looked at me. His eyes were the size of basketballs. I literally dropped Sly, and turned around, and looked at Belmont and smiled. Sly walked to the trailer and said, "We're on." They went on and did a fabulous show. I learned that trick from working with Graham, God rest his soul. There were times when you could turn the thing around with a good job of acting angry. We all owe tremendous debts to Bill, that being one of them.

The Who, still not in love with the idea that Peter had been talked into doing this by Frank and me, were quite exhausted and wanted to go

home. Their manager, John Wolf, stormed me and said, "If we don't get paid before we go on, we're not going on," and I said, "It doesn't say anything in the contract about this." "It doesn't say anything in the contract about going on eight hours late in the rain, either," he said. So I picked up the phone and called John Roberts. It was about eleven o'clock at night and I said, "John, I need the Who's money." John got a bank officer out of bed to open the bank and put somebody on a motorcycle to bring me the money so the band could go on stage.

Joe MacDonald played the first solo performance he'd ever played simply because, after Richie Havens, there was nobody else. I said, "Remember when we were in Amsterdam and we were talking about doing it on your own? Please!" I borrowed the first guitar I saw, slapped it into his hand, put my hand on the middle of his back, and shoved him on stage. He went out and was great. Those sorts of things happened.

Hendrix circled the festival for two days. We were unable to get him in and also to negotiate all the conditions that everybody wanted. Once Jimi actually went on stage, he was going to be the last act. It was four or five o'clock Monday morning, and I just went straight back to my trailer and laid down and went out like a light. I remember waking up hearing the first notes of "The Star-Spangled Banner."

I can honestly say I didn't have any drugs to assist me because I had enough adrenaline running to keep up half the world. I don't have any regrets about something that had such a great positive effect on me as a human being.

JOAN BAEZ (IN PRINT DRESS)

MELANIE

MICHAEL LANG
FESTIVAL EXECUTIVE PRODUCER

Woodstock was very much like we hoped it would be but much bigger. A lot of the work we did was to make sure that the feeling, once you arrived, was very much like what happened. We spent time making sure that things that were going wrong with other shows didn't go wrong with ours. I went to other events and saw the problems. There were a lot of riots and I saw that they were always setups by the security, and pre-planned confrontations, and it seemed really senseless to me. It was Stanley Goldstein's idea to have the Hog Farm as security, great idea.

We intended Woodstock to be a social statement. We designed it as a gathering of the tribes. We were trying to get all of the bands that had any relevance that year, and all of the people that you recognized every place that you went in the country, to come together and more or less see if they could live the idea—the dream. And it came pretty close.

In what way didn't it come close?

Monday morning everybody went back to their former lives, but I think everybody carried something with them, that they probably carry to this day—which was the knowledge that you can have that kind of feeling, that sense of community, that sense of togetherness with a massive amount of people that you really didn't know before. I think it gave everybody a lot of hope.

There were lots of things that made it special, but I think it was all born out of that same sense of community, the part of you that acts with helping your neighbor, pulling together, and dealing with natural adversities with a sense of community.

There was such an amazing feeling in the air, you could feel it on the Thruway, you could feel it on the roads leading to this thing, you could feel it for miles and miles. So much positive energy in one spot is an awesome thing.

We designed the festival so the music was no more or less important than any other element. The people were the stars, and bands are made up of people, so music was very much a part of it but no bigger part than anything else. The musicians were billed alphabetically so there were no stars. We really meant to focus on the whole event, not on any one thing, and that worked really well for us.

MIKE LANG (CENTER)

What was it like at age 24, being responsible for getting so many things done on an impossible schedule?

I had a great time. It was a chance to live out a dream—to make it a reality. It was a great experience for me. I guess I knew how all the pieces fit together, because I had an overview of it. You have to deal with the problems one by one, and not get too excited, otherwise you don't get through them. It's my nature to do whatever there is to be done. If you see things that are being left undone, you do them.

What were the best and worst things that happened?

The best thing that happened was everything that happened. The worst thing was the financial mess afterward, and the fact that the four of us who did Woodstock were really too young and immature to deal with it well. There was a lot of financial pressure, and it took a long time to work out.

Did you realize what was happening when it was happening—that it was going to last twenty-five years?

Well, you don't think in those terms, but you realize that something very extraordinary was happening, everybody realized that.

Did you fully realize your vision?

Yes, completely. We didn't go into it wanting to lose money, but in every other aspect it was certainly everything we wanted it to be. Jerry Garcia wrote in this book's introduction that it was like there was an extraterrestrial presence at Woodstock. Certainly a great spirit was watching over that site. Woodstock was definitely cosmic and magical.

LISA LAW
PHOTOGRAPHER AND MEMBER
of the Hog Farm

We were innocent flower children, living communally, sharing, playing music. We took mind-expanding drugs including marijuana. Music was taking a turn, expressing this new consciousness. Bob Dylan said, "The times they are a-changing." We all wanted to stop the war in Vietnam. Spiritual leaders were teaching the breath of fire and how to get in touch with our inner selves. We embraced the cultures of indigenous tribes, planted corn, lived in tepees that we made, and wore leather with fringe and beaded headbands. We were getting back to basics, rebelling against the status quo. We were "turning on, tuning in, and dropping out" and at the same time dropping back into society with a whole new twist: "Don't trash our Mother Earth, respect her. Be responsible human beings and come from a place of integrity and honesty."

In July 1969, Stan Goldstein, who was working for some promoters of a festival coming up in August, visited us at the Hog Farm in New Mexico. He was looking for a group of people to help him with the concert who had integrity and were part of the counterculture. We wanted to do it if we could do a free kitchen and take care of the fire trails, and Stan said we could. Volunteers from communes and local tribes poured down from the mountains of New Mexico, and we all crowded into buses for the ride to Albuquerque.

At the Albuquerque airport, while waiting for our jumbo jet to arrive, we took turns going to the bathroom to sip acid-tainted wine. Our tepee poles actually fit into the luggage compartment. During the flight the stewardesses were locked in the rest rooms, I think. Babies were running up and down the aisles.

At Kennedy Airport we were greeted by TV cameras and crews wanting to know if we were in charge of security. Wavy was shocked when he heard this, but he recovered quickly. "Do you feel secure?" he asked. "Yes," the reporter said. Then Wavy said, "See, it must be working." The news men hurriedly jotted it all down.

They ushered us into buses, and off we went to Bethel. Our buses, which had left New Mexico a week earlier, had arrived, and the crews were building the free stage. We put up a giant tepee that would be the PLEASE medical tent in our area, please being the word we used for "policing activities."

The advance crew had built a wooden dome, covered it with plastic, and set up a full kitchen. Max Yasgur provided us with milk, yogurt, and eggs. There was plenty of food, and we started feeding lines of early arrivals. These people were then given jobs helping to build forest trails and a jungle gym made out of logs and branches. A sandbox was constructed for kids.

Bonnie Jean Romney, Wavy's wife, was in charge of the kitchen and had gathered together pots and pans. We discussed just how much food would be needed and what we should serve. It was then that I realized (I do believe I got a direct message from God), that this was going to be bigger than any group we had fed before. We were going to need an immense amount of supplies.

Being well directed by the cosmic-powers-that-be, I approached John Morris and asked him for three thousand dollars. I guess I made a good case, as he gave me the cash with no hesitation, and to this day he tells the story of how I intimidated him more than anyone else in his life. Hog Farmer Peter White Rabbit and I pounded New York City streets for two days buying stainless-steel pots, utensils, and 160,000 paper plates. Then we ran out of money. The city festival office was just down the street. "Can I have another three thousand dollars?" I pleaded and went off again buying 1,500 pounds of bulgur wheat, 1,500 pounds of rolled oats, dried apricots, currants, honey, wheat germ, and huge kegs of soy sauce. In Chinatown I purchased a jade Buddha to protect and bless the kitchen.

We built a kitchen with lots of cutting and serving surfaces, and as soon as the five gas burners were set up, volunteers began to cook and never stopped until the concert was over. We made five serving booths that accommodated ten lines of people. For lunch and dinner we ate bulgur wheat with vegetables. Muesli was for breakfast, not very tasty but very nutritious. Being a health food nut, I figured nutrition was a major issue if one was going to be thrown against the elements. The elements showed up Friday night.

The stage was almost built and the fences were going up, but there were too many fences to be built and the turnstiles never got up. More and more people were camping out in the fields. They would walk right up to a fence, lay it down, and walk over it. Then they would plop themselves down on tarps, make a cushion of their sleeping bags, take off their tops to enjoy the sun, and stay there waiting for the music. There must have been fifty thousand of these squatters on the field by Friday morning. The promoters told my husband, Tom Law, and Wavy it was time to clear the fields and start taking tickets. Wavy said, "Do you want to have a good movie or a bad movie?" It became a free festival.

It was a tidal wave. People just kept coming. I stood up on top of the hill at the back of the stage and looked down the road and saw miles of cars parked on the shoulders of the road and six people abreast coming toward the field carrying clothes, coolers, and sleeping bags, big smiles on their faces.

What if all these people took acid at once? Yee gads! This could be a major problem. The Hogs got into a huddle and decided to put together a core of people who would take care of those Tripsters in need. They would be recognized by red cloth arm-

154

bands. By the end of the festival there must have been 200,000 people wearing the red armbands.

We helped medics set up their tents and erected "trip" tents next to theirs. If they got hold of a guy on acid, they would gingerly walk him to our tents instead of stopping his trip with Thorazine. Not good to stop in the middle, it can fuck with your reality the rest of your life. We shared with the Tripster the fact that he was on a trip and would come down soon, which he did.

The free stage by the Hog Farm camp had its own music and audience. Some people never saw the main stage. Pup tents, tepees, and campers lined the hillsides.

The festival chiefs had hired off-duty police to help with traffic and crowd control. They wore T-shirts that read, PLEASE FORCE. It was supposed to establish peaceful security. It worked. Everyone was helping everyone else keep their scene together.

It rained Friday night and all throughout the festival, on and off. Fields became mud slides. It would start to pour, and people would stand up and let the water run through their feet. Then they would sit down again, not wanting to leave their place lest they lose it. Everyone was sharing their food. All the concessions started giving away their food, and the National Guard dropped supplies from planes. I would go to a neighboring farm with a truck and buy whole rows of vegetables. Saturday morning after Tom Law taught yoga from the main stage, Wavy got up and said, "What we have in mind is breakfast in bed for four hundred thousand!" I then took the mike and told them where they could get this food. Realizing that lots of kids were not eating at all, we filled twenty-five new plastic trash cans with muesli mix and served it out of paper cups at the side of the stage along with cups of fresh water.

Once a day I would hail a helicopter, say I was with the Hog Farm, and get a lift into the sky. Yeaow, what a view! We had created our own city, half a million loving, sharing freaks. I could see the traffic for

miles. People were still coming. Traffic was backed up all the way to the interstate. The lake behind the stage was filled with naked bathers. Helicopters were everywhere, dropping off and picking up performers who had no other way to get into the festival.

I ordered a truckload of food to come in from a neighboring town. It took the driver nine hours to drive the normal twenty-minute run. What could I say to him when he piled out of the truck in a rage? "Here, have some dinner on us and relax, and we thank you from the bottoms of our bellies."

Sleep was the farthest thing from my mind. I think I got one hour a day. On Sunday I got my first shower when the Hog Farmers rigged up a hose that someone would hold at the top of a ladder and aim down on the naked bodies below.

I know there was music at Woodstock. They said Crosby, Stills and Nash played their second gig there, that Santana wooed the crowd. Richie Havens created "Freedom" right on stage when he ran out of songs. Country Joe MacDonald got the crowd to yell out F-U-C-K, and Jimi Hendrix played the national anthem and made that guitar sing like no one else had ever done. But for me Woodstock was the people, getting along, sharing, caring, doctoring, feeding. It was the first time we were in charge, and we showed the world what life could be like. We had created the Woodstock Generation. "We could change the world, rearrange the world," Graham Nash wrote. Can that feeling ever be re-created? I would like to think so. That is why over twenty million people today will tell you they were at Woodstock.

JOHN ROBERTS
FESTIVAL FINANCIER

Joel and I met Michael Lang and Artie Kornfeld in February 1969 when we were building a recording studio in Manhattan. A lawyer by the name of Miles Lury called us up and said he had a couple of clients who were interested in building a recording studio in Woodstock, and he wondered if we would share our experiences with them.

The most important thing about organizing the festival was to get the right security. Wes Pomeroy was a decent, lovely gentleman. I guess that you'd describe him as a humanist, which was a surprise considering he came from a law enforcement background. In 1969 there were two schools of law enforcement. One was "Cuff 'em, book, 'em, take 'em to jail," and the other was "Reason with them, find out what their problems are." Wes definitely came from that second school.

We initially hoped that we would get a major player like Restaurant Associates to handle the food concessions. But as our problems mounted as we changed sites, responsible food purveyors had doubts as to whether we were going to pull this thing off. So finally a friend of a friend said there are these guys who have some food experience and they'd be interested in doing this, and I said anyone who'd bring truckloads of hot dogs up there would be great. So that's how we met Food for Love.

We spent a great deal of time conceptualizing what we wanted to do. We came up with the concept of peace and music. And peace was not intended as some kind of codeword for "get out of Vietnam." Peace was a shorthand way of saying "a weekend of freedom from whatever is bothering you. Just come to the country and have a nice time."

Max Yasgur had been following the accounts of our battles in Walkill, and when we were thrown out, he called us. Mel and Michael went up to look at the land and called me and said you've got to

make a deal with this farmer. I hopped on my motorbike immediately. He was a delightful, charming guy, but he was also a businessman and he knew he had us over a barrel. We negotiated a deal with him for $50,000, plus we had to clean up. Max was an important person. He had a lot of good contacts, and since we felt we were going to generate some opposition once people realized what was going on, we moved forward with a surge of inevitability and hoped we might squeak through before the opposition could martial its forces and stop us. And that's in essence what happened.

We had one huge problem. We had sold about a million dollars worth of tickets for Wallkill, so we had to make sure everyone knew those tickets would be honored in White Lake. The press had been carrying accounts of how the festival was dead, so we had to counteract that. It was a nightmarish problem for roughly thirty days letting people know where the concert was going to be.

After the festival I was at the bank in New York talking to a bunch of panicked bankers when I got a call that a dead body had been found when they were cleaning up. The guy had been accidentally run over by the machinery that was compacting and gathering the trash. It was pretty emotional. Joel and I were both in the bank, and it felt like our world had collapsed. We had spent well in excess of a million dollars over the receipts. The newspaper accounts of Woodstock the morning after were not friendly. The New York Times had headlined it, NIGHTMARE IN THE CATSKILLS. We had bankers and creditors and just about everyone breathing down our necks and then the information that this boy had been killed accidentally at the site felt like the last straw. I remember feeling broken up about it.

The bank said they'd paid out a million dollars over the original $250,000 we had in our account but had no documentation to support it. We said it was our intention to honor these debts and we would

sign whatever papers were necessary. That was something that my father had always felt strongly about. You can regain lost money, but lost reputations are forever.

If we had had the hundred thousand people we were expecting, that would have been twenty to thirty thousand cars and we probably could have handled that without too much trouble because we had hundreds of acres of parking lots. But we had four to five times as many people, so we had many more cars. Also it rained, so many of the parking lots were a sea of mud. You couldn't drive in there.

We started getting reports that the surrounding community was very upset about long hair, drugs, what have you. You have to go back to 1969 and recall the temper of the times. People under twenty-five with long hair were widely suspected of all kinds of unnatural behavior by people over twenty-five with short hair, and we felt we didn't want to fuel those fires. So one of the things we asked people constructing the site was that they not use drugs and that they comport themselves in ways designed to reassure the local people.

What I recall vividly is around one o'clock Friday morning Joel and I decided to take a ride to visit the parking areas. Most of them were empty. At some point we crested a hill on our motorbikes. I can remember just looking out over the hills toward where the festival was and all I could see were campfires. I had the sense of this massive army before the battle, waiting there. And it reminded me of Henry V. It was a still, misty evening. Joel and I looked at each other with this—what's that great expression that Keats has?—with "a look of wild surmise." What does all this mean for us and what will the morrow bring? It was a wonderful moment that I'll always remember.

The Yasgurs were decent, gentle, caring people. They came to our rescue. There would have been no Woodstock without Max and Miriam Yasgur. When the festival was over and there was all this

trouble because of the dead boy, the lawsuits, the pillorying in the press, and the loss of money, the Yasgurs were steadfast friends. They didn't call up and say, "You didn't clean up this or that acre, you didn't do this or that," but "Anything we can do to help?" We did clean up their land. Max called me a month after the festival and said, "I can imagine what you're going through, I know you're only twenty four years old. You must be having a nightmare of a time. I have a great idea, why don't you come up here for a month and milk cows. You can forget about Woodstock for a month." I almost took him up on it, but I had met a girl at Woodstock, and my romance took precedence over milking cows. I married her.

From there Joel and I stayed in the music business; we remained and still are partners. We ran that recording studio and production company for the next ten years. We have been in the venture-capital business ever since. We are not really button-down types. We've gotten involved in dozens of strange, interesting ventures over the years. In fact things have come full circle—we're producing a twenty-fifth anniversary event in 1994. The world has changed a lot, and there are a lot of roadblocks in our way. But it's got a shot.

John Roberts passed away in 2001, thirty-two years after Woodstock, still married to Rona, the girl he met there.

HENRY DILTZ
ONE OF THE TWO OFFICIAL FESTIVAL PHOTOGRAPHERS

The first pictures I took of Woodstock were of Mel Lawrence looking at the rain out the window and talking on the telephone calling contractors. From there I followed him around. I saw where they were

JOHN FOGERTY, CREEDENCE CLEARWATER REVIVAL

going to put the water pipes, where people would be camping, having booths and concession stands. We walked through the woods to where the Hog Farm was going to be. This was all before anyone had arrived; it was just Mel and me walking through these green fields of alfalfa.

A few days later the Hog Farm arrived, and they set up their tepees and cook shacks. In the afternoons after work when it got real hot, they'd jump into their multicolored school bus and go swimming. Men, women, and lots of little kids would take off all their clothes and jump in the lake, about sixty of them.

The stage was under construction. There were hippie guys hammering nails with their shirts off, and there was this beautiful hill with waving green grass, alfalfa blowing in the wind, and blue sky. It was really beautiful.

At this point there was no urgency. It was like being at summer camp, just an idyllic summer afternoon in upstate New York. Hippie ladies would come in the afternoon with sandwiches and drinks for lunch for everyone, and they'd have a big picnic on the stage deck.

My job was to hang out and take pictures. I'd follow the art people around while they were painting big banners, and then I'd watch people do the wiring and carpentry. Everyone seemed busy but not frantic.

When the rain came, there was chaos. Everybody had ponchos on, trucks were getting stuck in the mud. Then the weather was nice for a long stretch of time.

I'd be taking pictures, and Michael Lang would come along on a motorcycle, a horse, or a tractor. Every time he'd have his leather vest on with his curly hair, and he was always very positive. Any time you'd ask him a question, he'd say, "Right, go for it, sure, fine." Everything was very pleasant, nobody was uptight, nobody was shouting orders, nobody was tense about anything. It was a real neat vibe.

Then things changed suddenly one afternoon. There was a small group of people sitting in this previously empty field. What were they doing here, watching us build? During the afternoon the crowd got a little larger, until there was quite a sizable group of people sitting there, and then you started to think, "Wait a minute, these people are here for the concert, and here we are, we're not even ready for them yet." Suddenly there was that feeling.

I made a trip to my boardinghouse in my station wagon. I didn't know it was going to be my last trip, but luckily I brought all my film back and I parked behind the stage. The following day I tried to go back to my room, but I couldn't, because the roads were totally plugged with cars. Cars would park on the shoulders of the road, so there was no way to go around. The roads became parking lots.

As the concert went on, it became hard to get on the stage, even though I had an access pass. If I would leave the stage for an hour to go photograph something else, by the time I came back, that pass was no good anymore, unless it had the purple star on it, say, and then you had to run off and find

MAX YASGUR, READY TO SPEAK TO THE AUDIENCE

the right person to give you the purple star, all of which took a lot of time. There were just so many people on the stage, they had to clear them off and just change the passes. The best place to take photos was right from the side of the stage, which was where I spent most of my time. I remember shooting Richie Havens, John Sebastian, and Joe Cocker. It was terrific to be there on stage able to shoot all those people.

WEARING AN OFFICIAL FESTIVAL PASS, DISTRIBUTING UNDERGROUND NEWSPAPERS

There was panic on stage when the winds were whipping up, since they were whipping these canvas things that they had tied up. It was like a ship with a storm suddenly coming on and the guys quickly furling the sails. Guys were scrambling around trying to cover amps and take down things that were in danger of blowing away, and everyone was hurriedly putting on ponchos, and then the rain came. It didn't really seem to affect the audience much—they just stayed there. At one point a bunch of the crew walked out to the edge of the stage and heaved beer cans into the audience, and I stood right next to them taking pictures. As I stood on the lip of the stage, I could see people for 180 degrees, the people went on forever—a sea of faces.

Jimi Hendrix played into the dawn the last day. A lot of people had left, but there was still a sizable crowd. It was a sea of mud. Belongings that had been left behind, parts of tents, blankets, soggy sleeping bags, paper, garbage everywhere. It looked like a Civil War battlefield. It went on for acres and acres. What had once been a beautiful hillside of blowing grass was just a mud hole.

When it was over, I was concerned about this huge bag of film. Nobody knew this was going to be a famous thing until we were right in the middle of it and saw the headlines in The New York Times and saw the aerial photographs. I remember racing into New York City, developing my film at a lab, and taking it to Life magazine.

MAX YASGUR
DAIRY FARMER—OWNER OF THE FESTIVAL SITE

"I'm a farmer. [audience cheers] I don't know how to speak to twenty people at one time, let alone a crowd like this, but I think you people have proven something to the world—not only to the Town of Bethel or Sullivan County or New York State; you've proven something to the world. This is the largest group of people ever assembled in one place. We have had no idea that there would be this size group and because of that you had quite a few inconveniences as far as water and food and so forth. Your producers have done a mammoth job to see that you're taken care of —they'd enjoy a vote of thanks. [applause] But, above that, the important thing that you've proven to the world is that a half a million kids — and I call you kids because I have children that are older than you are — a half million young people can get together and have three days of fun and music and have nothing **but** fun and music, and I God Bless You for it!"

MAX YASGUR, OWNER OF THE SITE, MARTIN SCORCESE (FILM CREW MEMBER) RETURNS THE PEACE SIGN

TIM HARDIN

BOB "THE BEAR" HITE, CANNED HEAT, EMBRACING AN AUDIENCE MEMBER WHO JUMPED UP ON STAGE

JOAN BAEZ, PREGNAN

RAVI
SHANKAR

JANIS JOPLIN

David Clayton-Thomas,
Blood, Sweat & Tears

Ten Years After

BEFORE THE RAIN

TARA ROBERTS
LONG TIME RESIDENT OF WOODSTOCK, NY (NOT RELATED TO JOHN ROBERTS)

Woodstock, long before the tourists and music, had a very big beat population. I remember, when I was growing up in the early sixties, Woodstock had guys hanging out on the street with no shirts and long hair and beads back when it was like really weird to see people like that. We grew up living next door to Bob Dylan and we would go over and and listen to him jamming with Joan Baez, Jimi Hendrix, and Janis Joplin. We didn't have the foggiest idea who they were but we enjoyed the music. Years later, in 1969, when I was twelve, I had a summer job working behind the counter at Cary's Deli. I asked my mom if I could go to the Woodstock Festival. She said no and that was the end of that. It was sixty miles away, but droves of kids came in, asking where the festival was, where they were going to sleep and eat, and where the bathrooms were. We didn't have bathrooms, free food, or free places to sleep, so there were all these kids with nowhere to go and no money. Lucky for me I worked for a very generous lunatic and we just fed people until we were out of food—we gave them sandwiches and stuff for free or for discounts, like a nickel. After the festival, we had a really high population of teenage runaways, so some people began **Family** to take care of the problem. (Forty years later, **Family of Woodstock** is Ulster County's largest social services agency.)

It seems to me that the festival idea started from Saturday-night sound-ins that were held at Pam Copeland's field. We'd go and see all of those rock greats jamming and playing, Janis Joplin, Bob Dylan, Jimi Hendrix and Richie Havens. I remember Jimi Hendrix and Janis Joplin most because their music was so intense. Michael Lang wanted to do the festival in Woodstock but the local noise ordinance stopped it from happening here.

Even though Woodstock had not been known before the sixties as a place where music was coming from, it was a well-known arts colony, home to many alternative lifestyles. In 1903 the Byrdcliffe Arts Colony was founded here with the intention of creating a Utopian society. They built houses for artists who lived and worked communally. Classical musicians and composers would come to Woodstock in the summer to perform at the The Maverick, a second arts community. So you had this group of artists, musicians, poets, and composers. I think that the festival was a natural metamorphosis of all of Woodstock's history—an accumulation of free and progressive thinkers and creative people.

LEE ERDMAN
ONSITE VIDEO
PROJECTION/CONSTRUCTION

Just a week before the start of the festival Mike Lang asked me to oversee the onsite video projection in conjunction with the Joshua Light show. The large crane which sat in the middle of the audience held the cameras for live video projection system not the documentary film as many thought. On the first night, we began projections behind Credence Clearwater and Janis Joplin. A storm suddenly descended upon the festival. The 60x20 foot video screen that was tightly suspended at the rear of the stage was buffeted by the high winds so we decided to perforate the screen to keep it stable. As soon as we began to punch the holes, the entire screen ripped apart and that ended the light show. I remember Josh White announcing from the stage that the "Light Show would have to continue in everyone's eyeballs."

HELICOPTER LANDING AREA

Swami Satchidananda, Ron & Valma Merrians

CHRIS LANGHART
PLANNED AND BUILT THE SITE

I was hired by Mike Lang to oversee the construction of the festival infrastructure, water supply and communication capabilities for what would become (for three days at least) the second largest city in the State of New York.

Every morning people began to appear in front of my trailer offering to work and Ann would take down their names as I picked them off. We would slowly gather the crew which grew from seven or eight to a hundred and

same positive outlook.

After the first day of the festival which was very sunny and hot, we nearly ran out of water but we were saved by having put water purification tablets in each pipe section so when we needed to pump more water from other areas such as the lake, where people were swimming, it arrived purified. This made the water taste terrible and so no one used much water during the first day. But after that it was OK. With the help of my college roommate who was employed by the telephone company and well versed in their rules and regulations, we were

THE WALKILL SITE

twenty five or a hundred and thirty by the time the concert actually went on. Every morning we just hired more people. Working with my young crew we had only two and a half weeks to install four water tanks, dig wells, lay pipe, bury wires and light the forrest. With little sleep, my team also built the site pavilions, bridge and some of the food facilities. We were drafting and planning what had to be done as we were doing it! One of the most joyous aspects of the entire experience was that we all were about the same age and had the

able to make them to install 100 lines seven miles to the middle of a corn field, over half of which were for pay phones. They became the only means of reporting the event live as it happened, since traffic made contact with the outside world impossible. These pay phones became the best publicity anyone could hope for. The news media was ready to turn the festival into the largest mess you could imagine—a horror show, but you can't contradict long queues of kids calling home all day and night saying,

"This is the most wonderful thing I've ever been at!" and "I'm alright, don't worry."

Mike wanted the stage to have a rustic look. The stage staff never thought much about how the roof was going to get put up. They only thought about what it was going to look like after it was all up. That's why the two cranes remained on both sides of the stage through the entire concert, because they could not get it strung up into a state where all the forces were balanced...without more time. So Chip's stage lighting mostly remained stuck under the stage except for the ten or twelve follow spots; all the light you see on that stage was from follow-spots. There weren't any back-lights or over-head lights used because the roof could hardly hold up a light show screen, let alone lighting equipment.

I got paged to see if I could solve a spot-light problem on the front scaffold and that's how I got to see the Crosby, Stills, Nash and Young set from the front. Mostly I was in the back doing things like keeping the performer's kitchen working, dealing with the bridge, worrying about the water, attending to medical etc. It was fun to see that one set from the front as I didn't get to see much else from the front.

Usually on a project, the biggest obstacles are money, time and knowing what "done" is. Nobody could tell you what the second largest city was supposed to look like, so who knew when it was finished. We made some planning mistakes. One of the worst things is that there aren't any interviews with the artists because the heliport was so near the artist pavilion that the noise from the helicopters obliterated the possibility of doing that, but by the time we built the heliport, there were so many people camping everywhere that you couldn't put it anywhere else. We didn't figure we were going to have the second largest helicopter fleet in the state of New York (aside from the state police) but throngs walking made the roads useless.

DODEE GIEBAS
DANCING SPIRIT IN THE AUDIENCE

I feel fortunate to have been part of that experience. A movement, started in the sixties, crystallized at that time and place. I will carry it in my heart and soul forever.

It was advertised as three days of peace and music—and it was. People came from all over North America, from the East Coast to the West Coast. I went with a group of thirty people from Pittsburgh. We rented a thirty-foot U-Haul and lined the inside with old mattresses. At twenty I was the oldest of the group and one of the only two girls.

After driving all night we spent our first day in the Woodstock vicinity in a traffic jam leading up to the grounds. It became a giant, slow-moving road party in a country setting. We could hear the music plainly five miles away. The acoustics were amazing, since the stage was built in a pasture where the land formed a natural amphitheater. Many people got out of their crowded vehicles and continued to the site on foot. Our huge, comfortable truck attracted many fans for a visit, and we shared whatever sustenance they may have had. We began to make new friends.

By the time we reached the festival grounds, the gate was down, and it was declared a free concert! We parked our truck in a field by an old hay barn. If it became too hot in the truck, we planned to camp in the hayloft. I never even saw the inside of that barn because my friend and I decided to camp in the rain directly in front of center stage. We told our group to meet us there in the morning. Our night was spent sitting on two sleeping bags in the mud, shivering as the cool rain fell. The fire we built of wood and pieces of trash was a small comfort.

In the morning we spread out our sleeping bags to hold our spot, and soon our friends began to arrive. The concert began again and went almost continuously for the next two days. I stayed in that spot for the duration, only leaving when necessary and once to cool off in a nearby pond.

I can't speak for everyone at Woodstock, but my group was there for the music. We were the "counterculture," the "underground," and the music was our voice. The musicians were our champions, chosen by us to sing of our ideals and lifestyle. We had everything from Country Joe and the Fish singing, "Give me an F, give me a U," etc., to Joan Baez's beautiful rendition of "Swing Low Sweet Chariot." Country Joe also sang in protest of the Vietnam War. We had Richie Havens crying out for "Freedom," a powerful song, and Joe Cocker getting by and getting high with "a little help from my friends." Canned Heat sang about getting back to basics, "going to the country where the water tastes like wine."

And of course, being the outcasts of society that we were, we all related to the blues that were played for us by Ten Years After, Paul Butterfield Blues Band, the great Johnny Winter, and the always fantastic Janis Joplin. There was also good listening music by Santana, a favorite of mine. Some were more entertaining such as Arlo Guthrie's story of Alice's Restaurant.

The Who played their complete rock opera, Tommy. They were the last group to play on the second day of the festival, and when Tommy triumphed at the end of the opera, the sun was rising behind the stage—very dramatic. Steam was rising off the drummer. All the bands played their hearts out for us; we, in our massive number, provided the ultimate gratification for them.

Drugs were a part of our lifestyle; there were songs about the drug experience. The Grateful Dead gave "High on Cocaine," and Jefferson Airplane offered their haunting "White Rabbit." We heard Jimi Hendrix's "Purple Haze," about lovin' life on LSD, "'Scuse me while I kiss the sky."

Yes, we used drugs; many abused drugs. Some took drugs just to "party." Others used drugs to escape the reality they couldn't face. Some of us were on a spiritual quest for the truth, and we used drugs as a means of breaking away the bonds of a false personality imposed upon us by society and our parents—a search for the essence of our being, not having found it in structured religion. But we found there was a price to pay for using drugs, and payment was extracted from us mentally and physically. Many couldn't afford to pay the price, and some lost their sanity or their lives.

But not at Woodstock! For those three days we triumphed. We were the counterculture, a minority, but at Woodstock we were half a million strong. We proved to ourselves and to the world that people can coexist in peace and harmony under the most adverse conditions. We withstood a seven-mile traffic jam, a severe electrical storm, intense heat and humidity, a shortage of food and water, lack of sleep, overcrowding, a lack of facilities—in a sea of mud there were smiles on our faces. Never before or since have I seen so many ear-to-ear grins. There was not one act of violence in the three days of Woodstock. Can you grasp the enormity of that?

You may or may not be familiar with the Greek concept of agape. It means selfless, unconditional, nonsexual love—universal love. It was present at Woodstock, I know, I was there, I felt it surrounding me. At one point a helicopter dropped thousands of daisies from the sky. The daisies twirled down, their little heads spinning like propellers. We caught them. Thousands of us stood with daisies in our hands. We were the "flower children" and it was our symbol—a symbol of gentleness and beauty. Incredible!

Hamburgers were also dropped from a helicopter. There weren't enough for everyone, so we shared. In fact everything was shared by all throughout the festival. It just happened that way. Whatever came your way, you took a bite or a sip of and passed it on. If you focused on one thing such as a sandwich, you could see it growing smaller as it zigzagged through the crowd. If there was a jug of wine, the level receded as it bobbed on its way. I had a variety of things come my way. I can remember a dill pickle, I took a bite and passed it on; marijuana, sandwiches, apples, beer, wine, water, soda. I wasn't hungry or thirsty the entire time I was there.

Every once in a while someone would strip and run through the crowd in a celebration of life and freedom; we thought it beautiful. Imagine—no embarrassment or false modesty, just love of life in its purest form. There was one guy who walked unclothed for two days carrying a sheep. He had a sign on his back: "Don't eat animals. They're our friends." An outsider probably would have viewed us as a dirty, sweaty mass of half-naked, drug-crazed hippies. We were "hip." I've been attempting to explain what that meant and what it felt like to be there, a part of the whole. It was beautiful, it was awesome, it was incredible. I kept thinking, "This can't really be happening. It's too good to be true. It must be a dream and I'm going to wake up."

We went to Woodstock for the music, and although the music was phenomenal, we found so much more—memories and good feelings to last a llifetime.

After Woodstock many of us became disillusioned. I chose to travel in search of life's mysteries. After years I realized that the world isn't ready for world peace or world government or even ecological appreciation. Humanity has not yet evolved to that level. The love I felt at Woodstock was a microcosm of future possibilities. My generation pointed the way; it's up to future generations to try to take us back to the Garden.

BARBARA RISSMAN
AN 18-YEAR OLD PILGRIM FROM
LONG ISLAND

We noticed these big full-page ads in The New York Times that said, "Three days of peace and music, at the Woodstock Festival." All these great musicians were going to be there. I was eighteen and had just graduated high school, and my friends and I really wanted to go. Of course we didn't have tickets. I told my parents that I was going to a concert in the Catskills and they said, "Fine, have a good time." We drove up there. The traffic was so backed up, we had to stop and leave our car on the Thruway. It was miles from the concert, so we just hopped on the roof of a car that was allowed to go through and just inched along having a great time.

We arrived that Friday night. It was pretty dark and we had missed the first night of the concert. There was just a field there, and we decided to put our sleeping bags down and go to sleep. We woke up in the middle of the night, as it was raining pretty hard and we were soaked. We had to find shelter. We saw a barn in the distance and headed toward it. When we got up there, there was a whole bunch of people hanging out, and they were really welcoming. They said, "Oh, come on in, there's room." They had food and they shared it with us. In the morning when we got up, the farmer was very nice. He came out and said, "You kids are welcome to stay and use the barn." He allowed us to use the bathrooms in the house and use the telephones to call our parents collect, and so I did and said everything was fine.

That morning we went to the concert grounds. The crowds of people everywhere were just unbelievable. There were babies running around naked and babies on their parents' shoulders, and there were drugs everywhere. People were passing joints around. I remember being warned about brown acid, but mostly there was a real feeling of warmth and connection between all the people. There were people selling things like jewelry, and people bathing in a stream and waterfalls. It was just wonderful being there.

During the day I remember seeing Joe Cocker playing, and then there was a big rainstorm and we all went for shelter. But Saturday night was beautiful. During the concert we were walking through crowds of people to get closer to the stage. It was so muddy that we sank down into mud up to our ankles. I remember taking my shoes off because mud was gushing inside them and it was very uncomfortable. It didn't matter, because my feet felt warm and squishy and it was fine.

Creedence Clearwater played, and it was sort of warming up, and the Who played, and things were getting hotter and hotter, and then when Sly and the Family Stone played, everyone was jumping up and saying, "I want to take you higher." The whole experience was about warmth and friendliness. Whoever had food just passed it around.

Joints got passed around, and there was this very good feeling. If you said, "Excuse me," and wanted to get up closer, nobody said, "Hey, I'm here first." Everybody was very polite.

Crosby, Stills and Nash played and that was great. Then Janis Joplin and we were sitting so close that you could see the beads of sweat flying off her as she sang, and it was incredible. When the Who played, they were throwing and breaking their instruments on stage, and the fringes on Roger Daltry's jacket were incredible.

No one slept, we went right through the whole night until dawn. Then as the morning came, Jefferson Airplane played as the sun was coming up, and it was really amazing.

Later we headed back toward the barn, but by this time there was no plumbing at all in the whole area. The farmer no longer could let us use the bathrooms. The whole area was overtaxed. The phones were dead. I don't think we brought food of our own, but it really wasn't a problem, because there was food. The Hog Farm was serving meals.

I spoke to and met people from all over the country. It was at that time that I realized that I had other possibilities, that I could've gone off to California. There was this feeling that you really didn't need money. I don't know how much I had with me, probably not more than twenty-five dollars. But somehow there was a feeling that you'd make it, that you'd be fine, and that you could really do something else and have a real adventure.

Sunday there was another great concert, and we spent the whole day there. Then, Monday morning, everybody had cleared out, but we heard some music. The barn wasn't that far from the field, so we walked up there. The field was now this vast open space, and there was just garbage strewn about. But when we got close, Jimi Hendrix was playing, and that was really amazing. I found a Woodstock book lying on the ground among the rubble, and I still have it today.

I had a fantastic time, it was a highlight of my life, one of the most wonderful experiences I have had. I was so happy that I went. Driving home, we were all so exhilarated and high, not from drugs but just from having been part of this experience. I haven't been back to Yasgur's farm since, but I now live in Woodstock.

That afternoon when I came home, my parents were frantic. They had been in a panic because they had been watching the news and they heard that Woodstock was declared a national disaster area, that people were dying, that there wasn't enough food, no plumbing, and there were all these drugs. My father was a dentist, and he said that he'd been working on a patient who said, "Any parent who let their kid go there should be shot." And my father said he just kept his mouth shut. My mother said, "You know, when you said you were going to a concert in the Catskills, I thought it was something like Tanglewood. I thought you were going to be having a picnic on the lawn." The media highlighted certain aspects, the death, the people who were having bad trips on acid, the mud. I realized how things could be really peaceful with everybody sharing a common goal but it would be portrayed very differently by the press. So my parents were very upset that I had gone, but I was elated. I'll always remember Woodstock.

WES POMEROY
FESTIVAL CHIEF OF SECURITY

In 1968 I was training chiefs of police how to deal with riot prevention and control. I went to Washington because Ramsey Clark asked me to be his special assistant. I had picked up a law degree at night school, so I was qualified for a Department of Justice job.

I finally resigned and started Pomeroy Associates. Not too long afterward Stan Goldstein came to see me to talk about a Woodstock festival he was involved with. After making sure the promoters had ideas that I agreed with about keeping the peace and that they expected no guns or billy clubs, I said, "I'll work with you." I didn't know I'd end up running it.

Of course Woodstock is a lot of things to a lot of people. It's several things to me too. But one thing it was, was a real test of logistical planning and implementation and coordination of some key things that we needed to have happen with some good people doing it.

The one thing that surprised me, and pleasantly so, was that I was the oldest guy in the whole thing, and at forty-nine years old I saw these young guys in their twenties who obviously knew so much. I very quickly learned to respect them for what they could do. They did incredible things.

Michael Lang was the first one I met. He was a very interesting guy. I'd met some people like him before, people who were beginning to say, "If it feels right, it's right." And I had come to respect that. I hadn't really adopted it myself, but I understood it.

John and Joel looked like establishment guys, but they obviously had enough vision and adventure to go along with this, because they were taking a hell of a risk, particularly John, because it was his money. I saw they knew what they were talking about. I could see

as they developed things, they were right on top of everything. I liked them both.

My fee was two hundred dollars a day and it looked like it might be a very interesting experience. However, it was important for me not to blow my career on what someone may have seen as a hippie adventure. After people got used to it, it didn't bother anybody much, except I'm sure I had a file with the FBI.

We began recruiting New York City police officers to work at the festival. They wouldn't be carrying weapons and they would be wearing a uniform that looked peaceful and not militant. We showed them the bellbottom jeans and the red shirt with the peace sign on the front and the dove on the back. We hired about 335 of them.

Just a few days before the concert the police commissioner of New York said no policemen could go. That caused some consternation. However, we had the Hog Farm, who had some very creative ideas concerning security . We also had cops who came up anyway and were willing to work but wouldn't give their names.

You know, I get a lot of kudos for the security, but everybody was working on security, the whole environment, it was all part of an interwoven dynamic.

After it was over, I would have liked to stay for another week, because we had a lot of cleaning up to do and we were just getting started.

John had really gone way over his credit line, and the manager of the local bank was so distraught, we were afraid he was going to commit suicide because he had extended so much credit to us. We had people coming in saying, "I have ten acres here and people have been tromping all over it," and we'd say, "What kind of crop did you have?" By the time we got through, we knew how to estimate an acre of alfalfa or corn. We were paying them off for as long as we had money. But the last money we had went to pay the doctors.

We had to reassure those who had worked for us, "We know who you are and you're going to be taken care of, don't worry." I was pretty confident that what I said was true. I didn't know how John was going to do it, but my assessment of him was that he would take care of folks he promised to pay, and he did.

ROB FREEMAN
SHIRTLESS MAN, AT RIGHT, WITH HAT

Like teenagers of any generation, I was really into the music of my day. Already a big fan of many of the prominent sixties artists featured in the *Woodstock Music and Arts Fair* promo that blanketed the counter-culture in the summer of '69, I was beyond excited at the prospect of experiencing so many of them together in one venue. My desire to attend was instantaneous, with never so much as a thought given to the prospects of hunger, exhaustion, getting rained on, or sitting in a mud puddle for three days. The motivation for going was pure and simple: it was all about the music! There had been other major music festivals throughout the sixties, but either I was too young at the time or they were too far away from my home for me to attend. Woodstock came along when I deemed myself old enough—I had just turned seventeen the month before!—and it was going to be held only a two to three hour drive from where I grew up in Allentown, Pennsylvania. But wanting to go and actually going were two different things. I don't think my parents, or anyone else for that matter, really knew just how much the world was about to change as a result of that weekend. In late August 1969, my mother was in California and claims she not have let me go into that "den of iniquity" had she been home. So it was left to my father to give me the requisite permission to go. He reluctantly gave me his blessing predicated upon my promise to remain drug-free while there, a promise that I upheld, by the way. So, at 4am on August 15th, together with two band-mates, off I went.

The first part of the drive took the expected two-plus hours, as we headed north out of Pennsylvania and up the New York Thruway. But as soon we hit Route 17B just outside of White Lake, congestion grew to unimaginable proportions, and traffic eventually ground to a standstill. It took over eight hours for us to creep the last half mile to the festival site. Once there, it took us

198

an additional couple of hours just to park. During the time we were stuck on Route 17B, we would take turns staying with the car as the others wandered up and down the road, which was packed with an endless sea of vehicles all facing the same direction across both lanes. We spent much of the time sitting on top of our car for a better vantage point, observing the hordes arriving by car, motorcycle, bicycle, and on foot. When it seemed like forward motion could be made, we'd release the parking brake and push the car, there being no need to turn on the engine. After drifting several feet forward, we'd stop and continue to sit again.

By late afternoon, we had made our way into the festival site and, amazingly, ended up fairly close to the stage, just below the stage-right sound tower. What ensued over the next couple of days defies description, but I'll share a few highlights:

First and foremost, there was the music! The movie soundtrack album only hints at the spectacular stream of performances that emanated from the stage, permeating the crowd with enchantment and awe.

Then there were the people, the so-called "Woodstock Generation." It was utterly amazing to be part of such a huge throng, which buzzed with the energy of so many peacefully enjoying the music and the scene. As I recall, people didn't tend to stay in the same place for very long. They would just drift around as if riding a slow-moving current. The group you might encounter in your immediate area would constantly be shifting. From time to time, people would come flying by overhead. Supported by the up-stretched arms of the crowd, one could travel hundreds of yards without ever touching the ground— and fly they did! At some point during the long, cold night, I joined a group that was huddled around several small fires to keep warm. I was surprised to see that they were burning their shoes and other pieces of clothing to keep the fires going.

Another notable highlight for me was

GARTH HUDSON, THE BAND

arriving at the festival site only to find that the gates and fences had been torn down and that Woodstock had been declared a "free concert." Though it cost me only $18 when originally purchased, my uncollected Woodstock three-day pass thus became one of my most cherished—and possibly most valuable—pieces of sixties memorabilia.

At one point I took a nearly six-hour "freak tour," an extended and surreal journey through the strange land that was Woodstock. My goal in leaving my buddies in the crowd and setting out on my own was to acquire food and drinks for us and to locate a proper bathroom. Yeah, sure! Along the way I encountered people bathing in rivers, communes serving free food, yoga practitioners, magicians and jugglers, all kinds of goings-on. Each scene had its own unique soundtrack wafting in from the stage somewhere beyond as if seeping through from another dimension. I seem to recall bringing back some warm water and cold hot dogs, but according to my friends, I returned empty-handed. I'm really not sure.

A high point of the weekend occurred when the sun rose just as The Who finished performing Tommy and Grace Slick announced "morning maniac music" as the Jefferson Airplane's upcoming set. It was a moment worthy of religious reverence.

Finally, one post-Woodstock highlight: getting back home and taking a wonderful, hot shower to remove three days' worth of sweat, encrusted mud, and spilled soda. Ahh!

Being immersed in that exciting procession of great musical acts and reveling in the feeling of solidarity among the crowd surely made an indelible impact on anyone who attended Woodstock. But I think it also made a significant impact on those who weren't there. From August 15 to August 17 in 1969, the world stopped to observe a diverse collection of seemingly aimless counter-culture misfits rise up and proclaim themselves the "Woodstock Na-

tion," a utopian community based on Peace and Love and their expression through music. There were no reported crimes at Woodstock. Compare that to what happened at Woodstock '99!

Could there ever be another true Woodstock? I've often wondered. The in-name-only incarnations of later years, even those put on by the original Woodstock promoters, all seemed to fall short in many ways. To begin with, the magic so present in the music of 1969 wasn't there, at least not to my seasoned ears. The sense of spontaneity and adventure surrounding the original Woodstock wasn't there either. Over the years, hippies and other sixties counter-culture elements had morphed into something completely other, so surely the crowds weren't the same. And those would-be Woodstocks seemed over-commercialized and tainted by corporate sponsorships. In short, and in my best Dylanese, "The times they've been a' changin'." But if there were to be another true Woodstock, one that I believed would be as innocent and honest as the '69 festival, I'd be the first in line to get a ticket…only this time, older and wiser, I'd take lots of wet naps with me.

A note on Elliott Landy's photo: If you've ever seen the movie *Woodstock*, you may recall when the crowd was told to "get down from those [sound] towers" for fear that they might be unsafe. Well, my buddies and I were among those who had climbed up the towers for a better view. As we were complying with the request to descend, Elliott snapped the iconic photograph in which I am prominently featured. Over the years, I've seen that photo in *Life* magazine, in promotional materials for the movie *Woodstock*, on billboards, and even on a London subway station wall. To this day, that photo elicits warmth in my heart and ranks among my fondest treasures from that era, right up there with my unused Woodstock ticket, the belt I wore in that photo, and my vinyl *Sgt. Pepper* album.

JOE COCKER

LYNDA LANDY
WRITER/EDITOR

For me, the road to Woodstock began with a barely audible 2am transatlantic phone call. I had been living and working in Paris, a city of young, spirited social revolutionaries whose youth had just begun to ingest the new musical vibrations that were pulsating across the Atlantic from the U.S. in waves of psychedelic colors. The voice at the other end of the line faded in and out but I gathered that there was going to be a big music festival somewhere in the Catskills and I would be a fool to miss it. In less than 12 hours I was on a plane headed to JFK with a tee shirt, an extra pair of undies, socks and my electric hair rollers. Little did I know the real journey was just beginning!

A friend met me at the airport and we headed north in his Chevy Impala. Once outside the confines of the city we purchased a canteen, small pup tent and filled a plastic cooler with enough food to last us for a day. We figured once we got settled on the festival grounds we would go into "town" and buy anything else we needed. I was hoping there would be a motel near the site where I could rent a room, take a shower and set my hair with those electric rollers I had carted all the way from Paris. Suffering from jet lag, I drifted off to sleep as the car sped northward. I awoke to the sound of honking horns. Our car was pitched at a strange angle on a roadside embankment and at first I thought we had been in some sort of accident. My friend

Me at Woodstock. My hair was much longer then!

was outside the car, talking with a group of people and I quickly scrambled out after him. Roads were closed we were told…too many cars up ahead…. just grab what you can and walk. No one knew how far we were from the festival site but I figured we were probably fairly close since it looked like the army of people ahead of us were queuing up at the main gate….five miles later we were still walking!

When we arrived at the festival site we were immediately engulfed in a sea of humanity…. young men and women, all shapes, all colors… happy, smiling faces…full of life, full of anticipation…..what a scene! We picked out a spot on the hill overlooking the stage and my friend went off to find some water for we had already used up our canteen supply on that long march to Yasgur's farm. It was the last I would see of him that weekend. Everyone was smoking weed and sharing. We were high on our surroundings, high on the music and well, just plain high. Right before it began to rain the first night, I traded my tent for 2 joints…a big mistake! Fortunately when the first drops began to fall some kind souls invited me to share their tent but there really wasn't any way of staying dry and we all spent the rest of the weekend mired in mud. I remember using my electric hair roller kit as a seat to keep me from sinking further into the mushy field (see, I knew they would come in handy!) I even rescued a few hair pins from the kit contents and passed them around as roach holders…a brilliant idea at the time.

The music! Oh, the music! It was fantastic. It was uplifting. It was passionate. The mutual love between us and the performers flowed back and forth, bringing us sheer joy and hope for the future. We were one with each other and the earth. When we ran out of food, the Hog Farm fed us…when we were soaked to the bone, someone offered a blanket and the warmth of a camp fire. We were making history and we were sending a message of freedom and unity to the world.

On Monday morning, after the last strains

of Hendrix's "Star Spangled Banner", we hugged each other one last time and started off in different directions. We never met again and, even though many years have passed, I would like those wonderful caring people with whom I shared such a life altering experience to know that I will always keep them in my heart as I continue life's journey. And…oh yes…..if you happen to stumble across a set of electric rollers while visiting the festival site in years to come, they belong to me!

ALLEN GORDON
WOODSTOCK RESIDENT,
PUBLISHED A NEW AGE NEWSPAPER,
THE WOODSTOCK AQUARIAN, IN 1968

I was drawn to live in Woodstock in 1967 because it was where Bob Dylan lived. Woodstock was becoming a mecca for the culture of the mid-60's. The Vietnam War, electronic transformation, and psychedelics were altering people's consciousness on a mass scale, and a lot of people were drawn to alternate lifestyles.

I met Michael Lang in Coconut Grove, Florida, where he owned the Head Shop. It was a time when people were being profoundly changed from what had been another way of looking at life that was more linear and materialistic. The Vietnam War created a great wave of protest in this country, and the desire to throw off a lot of the old values led to a collective feeling of love.

I went to see Michael about three weeks before the festival and asked him if I could get a ticket for the festival. I was very broke in those days. He said, "Sure, come down." I drove over, and he gave me a ticket, and I felt so lucky. We thought maybe fifty thousand people were going to come. I came there a week before the festival with three or four dozen people from Woodstock, who helped the Hog Farm set up the free kitchen. There was the Ohayo Mountain Commune, Robert DePew Reynolds, Chris Grodon, a whole cluster of people that were living in this nude psychedelic commune on the top of Ohayo Mountain, hidden way back off the road in a building owned by Jerry Shultz, the owner of Slugs in New York City.

Everybody sensed something big was about to happen, but no one knew the enormity of it. The town itself was burgeoning with music. I remember one night in Woodstock, Santana was at the Elephant Cafe, Van Morrison was singing at the Sled Hill Cafe, Johnny Winter was playing at the Cafe Espresso. Just before the festival Jimi Hendrix was practicing "The Star-Spangled Banner" at the Tinker Street Cinema and he played that at the festival. Odetta was in town, and Paul Butterfield was playing. I said, "God, look at this amazing place we're living in." I felt very privileged to be a part of this cultural renaissance.

I had a spiritual revelation, I saw the oneness of all life and thought the world itself was going to change radically because of that. As the years went by, I found that not so many people's lives were changed so profoundly as my own. Most people had reverted to the financial and economic pressures of everyday life.

Woodstock was a spiritual event of almost biblical proportions. Although the music was the billed attraction, the main thing was the way the vast majority of people acted toward one another. There seemed to be an infectious quality of bliss. It seemed like humanity was suspended in a different dimension for a while. Many people remember that, and although the media, when it was happening, tried to portray it as a catastrophe, everybody who was there laughed because it was just a giant party, and I don't mean a raucous party, but people found out that spontaneously they could get along well. There was a huge amount of humanity. People were able to interact with each other in a caring way.

Afterward people went to communes, they tried to make changes in their lives and do righteous things. I know some people whose lives are the fruits of those days. They've raised families and they're active in terms of trying to do good things to help change life in their environment and on the planet, and they lead good, wholesome lives.

They've explored their inner and spiritual life through meditation and other approaches to realization. So I see many people who were affected. On the other hand, there followed a lot of superficial New-Ageism stuff that took on a silly quality compared with the immensity of the transcendental energy at that time.

Aquarius is the symbol of the water bearer, of brotherhood, and that is still real. We are on that cusp, so to speak. We all knew back then that humanity and the planet was sick and that a great purging and purification was going to have to happen if mankind was to live in a more spiritual way. But first the old forces at play were still intact, they had to change, and that wouldn't be easy. So I think to a large degree we're still seeing that. Despite our collective vision of love, peace, and brotherhood back then, we're still living in the middle of a profoundly troubled world: the environmental problems, the way people relate to one another; the wars; the violence. Maybe people are going to have to get sick before they get well. But I think when we talk in terms of the New Age, we're not talking in terms of ten or twenty years, we're talking in terms of a hundred years at a time, just a blink of an eye on the face of eternity. A lot of people wanted it to happen next week.

Woodstock was like a cosmic blast, where we were reminded for a moment. I liken it to the movie Close Encounters of the Third Kind, where people were zapped by the light from these spaceships and driven to this place. They have to go, and nothing will stand in their way. In the end, where they're going turns out to be a lovely experience. At Woodstock it was a manifestation of the divine in humanity.

I'm skeptical about trying to re-create the concert. The big challenge is personal and global transformation. The only remedy for changing this planet is profoundly changing ourselves. So, however you get there, that should be, I feel, your pursuit in life.

212

GRACE SLICK

August 16, 1993

Dear Mr. Landy,

I am writing this letter to thank you very very very much for the poster and calendar.
The poster is hanging on the wall in my room. I look at it everyday, thinking how cool it would have been if I could have been there in 1969.
The calendar is also very very nice. My friends, who, like me, love the 60's, admire the stuff, wishing it was theirs.
I think if the people of my generation try we will be successful in bringing back the sandals, bellbottoms, tye dye, and the cool music of Bob Dylan, Grateful Dead, and Jimi Hendrix. Then we will be able to bring back the 60's and maybe repeat history by going back up to Woodstock and reliving the past.
The photos are very nice and it is like being there when I look at them!
So thank you again. I am very grateful for everything. I hope to meet you one day in the future, either in Woodstock or somewhere else.

Love and peace,

Tracy Campo (age 13)

Dear Tracy:

I was very touched by your letter and excited by the knowledge that there are many young people who, like yourself, intuitively understand and embrace the values of the Woodstock Generation. As much as I would like to be in the sixties again, I realize that we cannot bring back that time but, rather, must create a "sixties" of our own, learning from that generation and attempting to improve the future. Woodstock and the Sixties were indications of the way we, as humanity, could progress. It was a statement to all the disbelievers, that the world could be one, that with the collective energy formed by loving people, problems could be solved and disharmonies balanced.
The clothing and music you speak of are very wonderful. Certainly they reflect the freedom, positive spirit and easygoing essence of the time, but life must move on. Today there are many young musicians who are potentially as powerful as those you speak of and they too must be given a chance. Many fabulous musicians have simply not had the opportunity to make their work known.

JOAN BAEZ

Remember also the spiritual books, the metaphysical tomes which inspired the Woodstock Generation. Woodstock was a way of thinking and being, supported by many age-old schools of spiritual thought and practice. Its essence, peace and love, comes from within, and this is what you feel, and why you are so attracted to the time. It's very simple—when you embrace this spirit, you are happy. No matter what travails life brings, you are ready for them and you use them to grow, to bring you to the next place in your life.
So look not only to the past, to history, to the archives of record companies, but also to the clubs next door, to the places you can hear music, to yourself, and to the spirit of your own generation, where you may discover your own Bob Dylan or Jimi Hendrix, who although not sounding like them, will resonate the musical vibration you need to move happily in life.

Woodstock was a time of flowering. The festival was the apex of an energy form created by a lot of people who were unhappy with the way things were and who had a joint focus on making a better life. It was an example for future generations, not of something to re-create, but of the possibilities that can arise from a time and feeling, including your own.

Woodstock was an accident that was meant to be. The music was not what it was about. The fashion of the time was not what it was about. You were what it was about—you and every other well-meaning person who, although you were not yet born, intuitively understands the values and feelings that were present during the sixties. Love thy neighbor as your brother; trust in the flow of life—that whatever is happening is there for you to learn from; depend on being taken care of by life; share what you have; give what you can. It is for you and all the young people who want to listen that I dedicate this book, in hopes that it may inspire your thoughts and actions throughout your lives, just as the things I learned during this time have inspired mine.

Love and peace,
Elliott
(August, 1993)

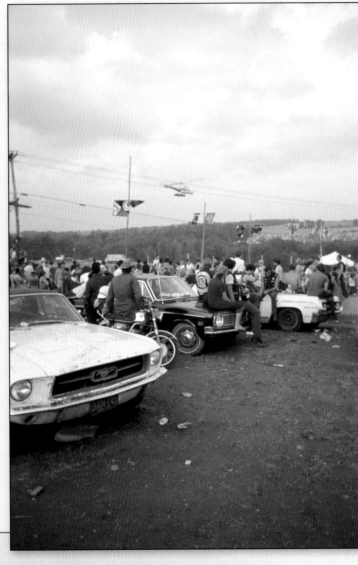

Woodstock was not about sex, drugs, and rock and roll. It was about spirituality, about love, about sharing, about helping each other, living in peace and harmony.

—Richie Havens

THE ESSENCE OF WOODSTOCK

—by Richie Havens

Woodstock started out as a normal festival. Most of us who had been booked to play there expected it to be just another festival, the kind popularized in the movie Monterey Pop, which had just been released.

The guy who drove us up to the site had hired twenty cars besides his own. We left very early that morning—around 5:30—and I was glad we did. I never would have made it there otherwise. There were two motels across the highway from each other, about seven miles away from the field, and we musicians stayed there and waited for the cars to come and take our equipment and gear to the field.

But when it came time for us to play, the road to get to the field was totally blocked by cars and people walking to the concert site, and there was no way to get the singers or the equipment to the stage.

We were already about an hour late when the first helicopter came down right outside my hotel window at the Howard Johnson's, and I was told that since I had the fewest instruments, I should go over first. It was a private helicopter. They had gotten some guy down the road who had a bubble helicopter, a big glass bubble, and he took us over. We packed into this bubble—two conga drums, two guitars, and three musicians, plus the pilot—and we just took off and headed for the field.

We flew over all of those people, and when I looked down at all the different colors, it looked like the world's largest Leroy Niemann painting. I said, "You know, this time they're not gonna be able to hide us. They're not gonna be able to make it look like a little thing." We had numbers this time. I could see that from the air.

This time we were going to make the news in a positive way.

We landed backstage. I was supposed to be fifth on the bill, but Michael Lang knew he had to get somebody onstage, since the bands with the big equipment couldn't get through, so I was the candidate.

He chased me around, and I finally consented to help him out and to go on first. But I told him, "The first beer can that comes up on stage, Michael, you're gonna owe me, 'cuz your concert is late, and they're gonna get me for it. Right?"

But fortunately people were so happy that something was gonna happen, that somebody was finally gonna play music, that they really were warm and welcoming to me as a musician. I had already made two albums, so I was fairly well known at that point. I went on stage and I started singing.

Two hours and forty minutes later, as I went off for the eighth time, they said, "No, go back, nobody else is here yet!" So I went back out for the eighth time, but I really didn't know what I was gonna sing. So I sat down on the stool, I strummed my guitar a little bit, I tuned up, and what happened was that I looked out over the crowd, and I saw the freedom that we thought we wanted to obtain being displayed right in front of me. We already had the freedom. And that was the essence of my experience, realizing that we were exercising this freedom that we had been trying to get since the early Sixties. So that's what I sang: "Freedom, freedom," just letting the word flow out over the crowd like that, over and over again.

The essence of Woodstock was not sex, drugs,

and rock and roll. That was the press's take on what happened there. The essence of Woodstock was bringing people of like mind together, into a place where they were gonna enjoy music, most of which they didn't even know and had never even heard before. But it wasn't just the music that brought them there. Woodstock was in essence a coming together, a gathering, a giant be-in. It was a people's festival, I would call it the first American people's festival, where the people came together to celebrate their essences, their concerns, and their feelings for the world around them.

So to me Woodstock had a very deep meaning. No one had ever seen 850,000 people get together in one field without having a riot. The essence of Woodstock was that we accomplished what we had started out to do in the early Sixties, which was to show that we, as young people, were not going to back down from our political feelings, our emotional feelings, and our newly discovered citizenry.

Rock 'n' roll was the first generational primal scream. Woodstock was an envelope of consciousness, a way of being. We had a different view of the world and we wanted people to know that the world wasn't as negative as most people thought—that there were a lot of positive things that we could make happen for the betterment of our planet and the world around us.

The world wasn't gonna change overnight. We never expected it to. To bring about the kind of changes we were looking for immediately, a flying saucer would have to land to scare us all into being one world. But I do think that the spirit of Woodstock has saturated the world just about, and has served the purpose of awakening minds to the fact that they, too, have the right to celebrate, they, too, have the right to have their own Woodstocks.

As far as I'm concerned, everyone now is a product of the Woodstock spirit, and there is no way they can get around it. Our doctors have been to Woodstock, our nurses have been to Woodstock, our lawyers have been to Woodstock. Even our judges and police—or at least some of them—have been to Woodstock. And little by little, that spirit — that sense of calm spirituality that came out of Woodstock and permeated our personalities—is very much alive and very much a part of our every day, our every moment.

ONE YEAR LATER

MOVING ON

While working with The Band and Dylan, I spent a lot of time in the town of Woodstock in upstate New York, fell in love with it, and decided to move there. I found a lovely house at the end of a dead-end road, exactly what I had been looking for.

Life was sweet. The spirituality of the place took me over and transformed my life. I grew tired of taking photographs of musicians and being involved with the music industry. I yearned to return to my original inspiration for taking photographs–to show beauty to people.

As a way of escaping from the commercial demands of photography, I opened a small gallery in Woodstock, with the intention of showing my photographs and paintings. During that period I discovered the world of metaphysics and spirituality. I found that many of the ancient wisdoms and Oriental health practices had validity for my life. I became totally fascinated with books such as the I Ching, the Edgar Cayce readings, Be Here Now, The Aquarian Gospel of Jesus The Christ, The Urantia Book, the Tao Te Ching, Talks by Krishnamurti, books on astrology, the tarot, the kabala, natural health care, macrobiotics, yoga, tai chi, etc. I felt that people should know about these things, and the gallery turned into a metaphysical bookshop as I followed my passion.

I was happy to sit in the bookshop and talk with people who came by but whenever I was recognized as "Elliott Landy, the photographer," I quickly changed the conversation. I wanted to be related to for who I was, not for my connection to famous people, and I wasn't interested in exhibiting or talking about my music photographs. In order to move on to another period of my life and art, I had to free my mind and dissociate myself from my previous success.

I wanted to photograph what I found beautiful in the normal course of my own life, not what was shown to me through media. I was through photographing someone else's art form or someone else's war. This period of totally personal photography began with pictures of my newly born daughter and continued for seven years on the road in Europe, where we lived and traveled in a forty-passenger bus. During this time I was inspired by the beauty of my children and wanted to share it with others. I tried to make people aware of the importance of children and family life through my photographs of innocence and love.

After the children began to grow up, my photography became more experimental and abstract, although I occasionally did jobs in the music business when someone found me.

Today in addition to photographing an occasional musician who inspires or pays me, I continue to work with children, multiple imagery, motion, and kaleidoscopic lenses to create images which reflect purity, innocence, and non-attachment to perceived normal reality. I feel it is important, that people have a vision of life which allows more hope and more opportunity than are available in the images presented by newspapers and television.

In 1970 I discovered a style of combining moving images with music so that the motion of the images was syncopated with the rhythms of the music. This visual music work forms the basis of an interactive music-visual system I am developing today

Life is good, I'm living in Woodstock again with a wonderful lady in a beautiful home with a view of the mountains, caretaking my vintage work. But sometimes I find myself wishing I could find something that would involve me as totally as still photography did in years past. At 50 I still feel young, but I don't have the need to do art anymore. If I want to, that's fine, but I don't need to, like I did.

Recently I saw my old photo-credit stamp on the back of a print, and it brought that feeling of total immersion back to me: I lived in two and a half rooms at 88th St. and Broadway in New York City, in a street-level apartment with soot-covered windows and car noise outside.

I lived there until I met Bob Dylan and The Band and decided to move to Woodstock. By that time I had taken many of the photos which today are history to a new generation.

In those days there was nothing else. Shoot, go home to process the film, go out and shoot some more, give the prints to the newspaper, and do more. I loved doing pictures and having them published right away in the newspapers I was working with. No hassle, no wait, no pay. But what joy. To do work and see it in a place where others could see it too.

Eventually the business of rock 'n' roll photography turned me off. I gave my heart, and the people who wrote the checks never appreciated it, and people who had no vision usually controlled the artwork. Perhaps I'll find some way to get back to it someday—to do work and show it to people in a pure way, not one dictated by someone's imagined commercial needs.

My success with The Band and Dylan came because Albert Grossman used his leverage to take control of the album-cover process. Only

JOIWIND, SPAIN, '73

the artistic inspiration which bounced back and forth between the musicians and myself determined which pictures would be used. It was fun.

These are pictures of what was, of people like myself who were doing things because they loved to do them. It was "groovy," as we used to say, doing what we loved, but also we had no choice—we had to, our inner needs were too strong. And they still are.

So when I saw the photo-credit stamp with my old address on it, I realized that most of my famous photographs were taken while I was living in a near dungeon of a place, but to me it felt like heaven. My darkroom was an eight-foot sink

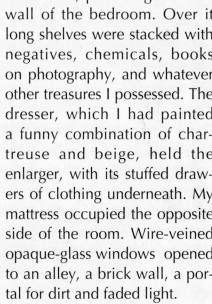

I had built, placed against one wall of the bedroom. Over it long shelves were stacked with negatives, chemicals, books on photography, and whatever other treasures I possessed. The dresser, which I had painted a funny combination of chartreuse and beige, held the enlarger, with its stuffed drawers of clothing underneath. My mattress occupied the opposite side of the room. Wire-veined opaque-glass windows opened to an alley, a brick wall, a portal for dirt and faded light.

But in that room, in that atmosphere, I was ecstatic, printing from late nights till early mornings, listening to Bob Fass on WBAI playing "Light My Fire," and occasionally calling him up with news from the underground. How can I describe it? Innocence, belief, faith? I felt I was part of something that was changing the world. I was right, and I was wrong—it didn't happen as fast as I thought it would, but it is still happening.

—ELLIOTT LANDY, WOODSTOCK, NY, 1994

MY GRATITUDE TO:

Lisette Modell, my first photography teacher, whose appreciation for my early photographs gave me the confidence to do more.

Larence Shustak, for teaching me the art of photography and the attitude of life and for the continuing inspiration his abandoned photographs provide.

Peter Moore, photographer, whose humble manner and sweet disposition taught me much.

Pat Dingle for being my partner in stories for the Underground Press.

Bob Fass, Steve Post, and WBAI of the late sixties for inspiring me through the long nights of printing..

Leslie Landy, who helped me escape to a better place in life; and for coloring my photos.

All my friends and co-conspirators from the sixties.

Jim Ferretti for being the generous master of so many things. Our collaborations will wait til another life.

Andras Nevai for being the spiritual guide that he is and for selflessly supporting my new art form.

Annette Maxberry for always being there for me and many others.

Werner Mark Linz of Continuum for publishing the first version of this book (1994)

Alice Linz, who had the vision to mention me to her father.

Diana Oestreich for editing the Woodstock interviews and helping me along my path.

Rob Baker for his editorial guidance.

Kelly Sinclair for helping me organize and evaluate my work.

Carita Lahdeniitty for her masterful digital printing and organizing my archive.

Grazyna Kleinman, my master darkroom printer.

Ryan Reich for his asistance with many things.

John Cerullo for saying *yes* to this book.

Randy and Barbara Rissman and Michele Slung, for their friendship.

(and again to Lynda Landy, thank you for more)

JOIWIND AND LESLIE, SPAIN, '73